PET
SOUNDS

* * *

New & Improved Stories from
The QC Report

QUINN CUMMINGS

ISBN: 978-0-9894473-0-0

This book is dedicated to every animal who has padded through my life.

I am better for having known you.

CONTENTS

WELCOME TO THE JUNGLE

One afternoon many years ago, my father called my mother from his office. One of his employees had come to work with a box of kittens — recent orphans of an ill-timed moving van. They were two weeks old and would need to be bottle-fed.

"Do you want one?" he asked.

This was a ludicrous question. At the time I was also two weeks old, and my mother was still trying to figure out how to change diapers while sleeping. No sane individual would even entertain this thought.

"What color are they?" she asked.

The colors of that litter are lost to history but I know for certain there was at least one tuxedo. Pooh and I were not only on the same feeding schedule, we apparently both enjoyed the same formula. I've never asked, but I like to think we had separate bottles. Whatever Pooh didn't want went to the family dog, a half-coyote/half-German Shepherd named

Ginger, who viewed us for the duration of her long life as beloved but not terribly bright puppies. I've seen pictures of the three of us together—a mid-century-modern tableau of Romulus, Remus and their wolf-mom. We all appear to be quite happy.

I never stood a chance.

For my entire life, with the exception of one year, there have always been animals under my roof. I've regretted places I've lived, shoes I've bought and nearly everyone I've dated, but I've never regretted a single animal I'd spontaneously decided to adopt. And it's always spontaneous; the pet version of getting knocked-up. I'll be driving along a city street, assuming the day is filled with errands and carbohydrates when suddenly I'm heading to the nearest pet store to grab bubble bath and Frontline for some filthy-yet-cheerful critter I've just extricated from a dumpster.

Every other life decision I fret over, whine about, ruminate upon, write pro-and-con lists for and then generally do nothing about. But pets exist in my experience to remind me of life's greater truths: stuff happens; roll with it; everything will work out; and don't forget the water bowl.

LOVE MACHINE

The cat thinks she's in love, but I suspect it's mostly physical.

Like all cats for whom I've had the privilege of buying smelly food, Lulabelle becomes fixated upon sleeping in very specific places. You'd think if you spent two-thirds of your life in a REM cycle you wouldn't be so picky about where you did your sleeping but every cat I've known has obsessed on a special place to sleep. And only that place will do. Until it doesn't.

For seven days, that special slumbering spot might be draped precariously over the back of a dining room chair— it's where all the fashionable cats snore. Then, on day eight, that same cat will avoid that same chair as if it were crawling with yappy, barf-dipped Chihuahuas. For the next three days, where's the trendiest feline nightspot? Why, everyone knows it's in the closet, dozing with your head shoved into a ripe Converse high-top! From there, who knows? What makes a sleeping place desirable to a cat is as plain to them as it is opaque to the large, food-serving, hominid slaves who lumber around the house. Mostly, I let Lulabelle be Lulabelle. The exceptions would include that time her chic resting place was splayed across a pound of imported Cheddar.

About two weeks ago, Consort went into the office to check the forty work emails that had accumulated since he'd gone to lunch. First I heard the surprised yelp, then I heard "Quinn...?" in the rising tone that could be correctly interpreted as *Please come attend to something. It's weird, and it's yours.*

I hear that tone a lot.

I went into the office and saw Consort pointing into a shadowy corner of the desk where all the extra bits of the computer live: modems, hard drives and stuff. I saw only shadow. Then I saw yellow eyes in the shadow. Lulabelle had crammed herself into a space about 60% of her girth and gone to sleep. Unaware of her presence, Consort sat at the desk and began to type. This must have awakened her and caused her to glare out at him from the adjacent depths, which I'm sure triggered a nice workout for his adrenal glands. I reached into the shelf, pulled out a protesting Lu, and carried her back to her favorite sleeping place from just that morning: under the bedroom bench, known locally as the Bench of Random Objects. She snarled at me and ran off into the house. By the time Consort checked in after a short break to see if any of the forty work emails he'd responded to had responded back, Lulabelle was once again huddled in the dark corner of the desk.

Between Consort and me, someone is on the computer at least half of the time we're home and, over the past month, the cat is almost always in her new favorite spot. This is a record stretch. After the first few days, whenever one of us sat down we'd automatically reach into the small space and extract the cat. After about a week, once it was confirmed her fur couldn't harm the delicate electronic gizmos, Consort and I simply gave up. It was puzzling, though. She was well past her usual "Moving On" date with regard to a sleeping spot and yet she showed no signs of relocating her naps to, say, the towel hamper or a soup tureen. Once, when moving her, I happened to put my hand in the spot where she slept. The external hard drive was comfortably warm and vibrated slightly.

I was charmed. I called Consort in so he could be charmed, too.

"She loves it because it reminds her of her mother!"

Consort put his hand on it. He said dryly, "Or it's a kitty marital aid."

AUGH! NO LONGER CHARMED!

My first instinct was to deny this accusation outright but the more I thought about it, the more I'd been forced to consider the new reality. Lulabelle spends extended periods of time with her new friend. When she finally deigns to come out, she is in a fabulous mood, purring furiously and courting my attention. This is the same cat that normally treats us like roommates arbitrarily assigned by the dorm manager until sophomore year when she can move off campus to live with the cool drama majors. I thought we were growing on her. It turns out, her electrical friend puts her in such a good mood even we can't harsh her mellow.

The good news: it seems her affections can't hurt the hard drive. Consort was concerned it might overheat but that seems to be when she gets up and leaves for a few minutes. I'm not sure the equipment is consenting but I'm not sure it *isn't* consenting. The activity in which she participates is legal in all fifty states, if for no other reason than she might be the first cat to conceive of it. All in all, this appears to be a happy and harmless activity.

But mark my words, I'm not paying for a wedding.

NO MORE WORDS AND NO MORE PROMISES

Here's a conversation I dearly wish could take place between me and the dog:

QUINN: Polly, we need to talk about your nighttime friends.

POLLY: You mean the special cats?

QUINN: Exactly.

POLLY: I love the special cats!

QUINN: Those aren't cats. Cats don't appear only at night. Cats don't have a white stripe running down their backs. When a large, affable dog such as you bumbles up to them, cats don't raise their tails and saturate the dog in breathtakingly foul-smelling oil.

Polly thinks a moment.

POLLY: What are you saying?

QUINN: Okay. If I promise to set up play-dates with Petunia (the pug next door) and Dolce & Gabbana (the Boston terriers up the block), and maybe throw in a couple of pig's ears every week, could you possibly stop making yourself the recruiting poster for animal HAZMAT?

POLLY: You bet.

That conversation would be sweet. I also think it would be sweet if Polly could carry her own poop bags and use them as needed. Sometimes I think we keep her around because it comforts us humans to know that no matter what we do, we are still not the dumbest mammals in the house.

Late Saturday night, I woke from a sound sleep to Consort shouting "Oh NO! YOU [expletive deleted] IDIOT!" followed immediately by the sounds of Polly being dragged to back door, the back door being opened, Polly being ejected and the back door being slammed. Hard.

I decided it was wise to get up. I emerged from the bedroom hallway into a solid wall of vile odor. Consort was returning from the laundry room with a towel over his nose.

"She got skunked?" I inquired, groggily.

Consort shot me a piercing look that said: *For the sake of our child and our future together, I'm going to ignore that question.*

Pointing to a pattern of yellowish drops on the hardwood floor, he explained, "She had to go out. I let her out. She must have gotten *this* close to the skunk because she was dripping stink-oil all the way across the damn house."

This is one of those situations where being physically defective comes in handy. Remember the weird kid from grade school that walked around half the year with a Kleenex permanently attached to her nose? The one who had laminated doctor's notes excusing her from outdoor exercise? I was that kid. Thanks to a lifetime of sinus problems my current nose has only two gears: 1) There is a smell present; and 2) There is no smell. I don't recognize big smell versus little smell. This is why I am not allowed to apply my own perfume.

So, while Consort was gagging and retching and clawing at the windows, my brain was saying, "Skunk... Huh... You might want to do something about that."

I sent Consort to the bedroom, opened all the windows and washed the skunk-saturated side of the house in Murphy's Oil soap. I waited twenty minutes and washed the floor once again. Twenty minutes later, I invited Consort back out into the main part of the house. He stuck his nose in nervously.

"So," I asked. "Any better?"

He sniffed.

"It's like..." he said cautiously, kindly not wanting to dismiss my post-midnight mop marathon. "...It's like a skunk. A skunk with a pine-scented urinal cake around its neck."

I sent him back to the bedroom and washed the floor again, this time with vinegar-based solution. Consort was recalled. He sniffed.

"Now it's a skunk making Easter eggs."

I dismissed him and lit some lavender and jasmine candles. I called Consort back.

"A skunk having a massage? Maybe a little Wyndham Hill music might help?"

I gave up, put Polly in the garage for the night and went to bed.

If I wanted to be a positive sort of person, I could focus on how our Polly tends to be an eager-to-please pet. Granted, she only has seven brain cells, two of which are dedicated to eating Kleenex, but when she does something wrong she looks appropriately abashed. She has no idea what just went wrong or how to avoid doing it again, and yet my standing there shouting in her direction makes her manifest some form of canine guilt. I know this because she gets this "guilty eyebrow" thing — an expression of such pure, pitiful sorrow and self-loathing I lack the literary skills to describe it. You're simply going to have to take my word on this.

The cat is a whole different story. I guess being a completely different species might have something to do with it. The cat and I could have had the following conversation this weekend:

INT. LIVING ROOM. Cat is grooming her abdomen. Quinn walks in and sits down on the couch next to cat.

QUINN: Lulabelle, we need to talk. I found another one today. You're out of control. You need to recognize this. You need help.

Quinn waits. Cat continues grooming. After a minute or so, cat looks up.

CAT: Oh, hey. When did you get here? Shouldn't you be pouring out kitty stars or something?

QUINN: No, we're not talking about food right now. We're talking about birds. Birds in my house. Baby birds. Elderly birds. Wounded birds. Dead birds. And what appeared to be a Cessna. You have to stop this.

Cat has fixated on removing something from between her toes. After a while, she glances at Quinn.

CAT: You like it well enough when I kill mice and rats.

QUINN: Yes, because they are vermin. They eat our food. They poop tiny cigars. They spread plague. Birds are pretty much harmless.

CAT: Tell you what. I'll tear the wings off the birds, and you can pretend they're mice.

QUINN: That's it. I'm getting you into rehab.

CAT: Fine. I'll kill all *their* birds. Then they'll send me back here and I'll do something unspeakable in your closet.

Lu is a portly, middle-aged cat. After my having to be nursemaid to one bird-offering and mortician to the rest, I belled her—which, to those of you who are too smart to own a cat, means I attached a little bell on her collar. In theory, this gives the birds enough time to hear her and, I don't know, fly away or get ready to apply a roundhouse kick. That's the theory. In practice, Lu merely considers the bell a sporting handicap and continues to stalk and capture birds with élan.

I'm not a fan of indoor/outdoor cats, especially in my neighborhood where if a car doesn't get the pet the coyotes will. Lulabelle came to us as an adult, having already been connected with two other families on the block (I think she arrives in the Welcome Wagon gift basket) and she has *always* been an indoor/outdoor cat. There are just so many times you can fling yourself between the cat and the front door as if saving a fellow soldier from a live grenade before you start to say, "Fine! Go outside. See if I care!" So she goes outside and a few hours later I learn she's brought her work home with her and, on at least one occasion, left it in my purse.

So, in sum, the facts are as follows:

Polly will continue to get crop-dusted by skunks. I will eventually decide it's cheaper to have a dog-groomer live with us full-time.

The cat will not only not stop killing birds but eventually will be cited by the US Forest Service for having brought down an endangered California Condor, which she will leave in my purse.

Knowing all of this, I will not give these pets away.

And I take back what I said earlier about Polly being the dumbest mammal in the house.

STRAY CAT STRUT

We have a suitor hanging around the house these days.

He's not exactly my type but he has an undeniable muscular charm and bad-boy appeal. While Consort and I are clearly not his reason for hanging around, he shows us a certain polite deference and is positively courtly in his attention towards his beloved. In fact, if it weren't for the urinating and the vomiting, I'd say he was the perfect first boyfriend.

About three months ago, Consort came in from the garage looking a touch confused.

"Quinn, how many cats do we have again?"

"We have one."

"She's black, right?"

It turned out that when Consort opened the back door, a cat flashed past him heading outside. Benumbed as he is to pets at this point, it only occurred to him after the fact that it was the wrong color. I was just grateful that it wasn't a Special Cat and I started closing the cat door after dusk. One morning, about a week later, Daughter went into the laundry room, and came flying back out announcing joyously "We have a new cat! She's gray and she wants to sleep on my bed!"

I slipped quickly into the back room and there, eating Lulabelle's food, was a large, gray, good-looking cat. It eyed me coolly.

"Hi." I said tentatively. "This is a little awkward, but who are you?"

In answer, it jumped to the floor and he (for it was clearly a he) swaggered out of the house. It was only then I noticed Lu, who must have been sharing the food bowl with him. She shot me a filthy sidelong glance and followed him outside. Like it's *my* fault she invited him for dinner and forgot to mention she had roommates.

We got plenty of chances to get to know about Rhett, as I have come to call him. Besides being handsome and brimming with self-confidence, he has a darker patch of fur right above his lip that resembles a moustache and would seem remarkably natural gracing a white linen suit. He spends his mornings with us. Actually, I usually find him sleeping on the newspaper when I go outside to pick it up, where he accepts a scratch on the head. He and Lu then spend the morning sleeping in total harmony in the back yard, flicking their tails in a synchronized manner. According to neighbors who are feeding him, he is one of the countless descendants of several feral cats in the neighborhood, most of whom are reflexively timid. Rhett, however, got the personality all the others lack, which has led to multiple feeding stations, two cats beds at different locations, and the love of a good cat/woman. Lulabelle—whom I have seen run a pit bull off the property with a look—seems to adore him.

But no relationship is without its drama. Ours comes in the form of a skinny tabby I've been told is named Tiger. Tiger either worships Lu or despises Rhett because at least twice a week he is in our yard, where he and Rhett stand about eight inches apart and scream abuse at each other. I dubbed it "The Male Cat Pointless Gargling Variety Hour." One of the times this happened, the noise seemed louder and more belligerent than usual. I walked towards the back door to shoo them out of the yard only to discover the show had gone on—or off—the road. Rhett and Tiger had moved their battle into the back room.

"Okay, THAT'S IT! Have you two even noticed she's *FIXED?*" I shouted, hustling them out the door with my foot. Each time I would stop herding them, they would take their fighting positions and start trash-talking all over again. I got them outside and the screaming didn't stop. I moved them to the back gate and the screaming didn't stop. I grabbed a broom and moved them through the gate and tried to get one to head one direction, one the other direction, with very little success. I add all this in case any neighbor saw me yelling and appearing to sweep cats up the sidewalk.

I came back in the house and found Lu sleeping on the couch.

"This is your fault, you know." I said accusingly.

She flicked an ear indifferently.

It was at that point I decided to nip this problem in the bud, as it were. Rhett would be neutered. It was the appropriate thing to do, what with the world in general and my neighborhood in particular being overrun with unwanted cats. Also, post-surgery, he wouldn't have to dominate every feline situation and might settle down with one of the nice older ladies who live near our house, instead of roaming his three zip-code turf. I found a low-cost spay/neuter program through the city and made an appointment. I couldn't keep him in the house overnight until his appointment due to his loathing of Polly, and the whole "Testicles make me want to leave an odor on fabric" issue, but this shouldn't be a problem, I thought, as he can be found every morning keeping our *Los Angeles Times* safe from other cats.

The morning of his clippage, Rhett was nowhere to be seen. I shook a bowl of food in a hopeful and seductive manner outside, and got nothing but Polly standing next to me making expectant eyes. I called the vet's office and cancelled my appointment.

The next morning, Rhett was back on the paper. I called the vet's office and took the first available appointment, which was the following morning.

The following morning, no Rhett. Once again, I cancelled the appointment. This time he didn't even bother to wait until the next day, but drifted by that evening to look at me through the open kitchen window. I considered him.

"You know, you'll feel better afterwards. Tiger won't irritate you as much."

He eyed me enigmatically.

"If you roam less, you might actually live to see another year."

He commenced to grooming his tail.

"We can tell everyone you were just in for a torn hamstring."

He leapt down and walked away, the symbols of his probably brief and tumultuous life mocking me as he walked.

Later that night, I was talking to an old friend, getting caught up.

"Jeremy is making me crazy." she sighed as I heard kids screaming in the background at her house "We've had three kids, which is all we ever wanted, and now he won't get a vasectomy like he promised."

"What does he say?"

"Oh, he doesn't say anything. I just keep making appointments for him to see the urologist and he claims he keeps 'forgetting' to go to them."

Rhett, may I introduce you to Jeremy. You're probably both hiding under the same house.

STUCK IN THE MIDDLE OF NOWHERE

I really dislike Halloween.

I dislike feeding complete strangers who drive to our neighborhood from miles away because they heard the pickings were easy.

I dislike handing out candy to an invading horde of sugar-addled delinquents who view their only role in this ceremony as grabbing candy from my hand and walking away in silence. In fairness, some of the children say "thank you" without prompting and some say "thank you" after gentle coaxing from their parent. But all too often, we have the following interaction:

ANGLE, FRONT DOOR. NIGHT. Child grabs fistfuls of candy from my bowl. I gently remove all but the first eight pieces. He turns to walk away.

QUINN: What do you say?

The boy and his mother stare at one another, stumped.

BOY: Uh...Abracadabra?

I guess they got *a* magic word and *the* magic word confused.

This all makes me just a bit more worried about the future of society. Usually, by the third hour of trick-or-treating, I am sitting on the couch anxiously waiting for the doorbell to ring and scarfing down cheap chocolate by the handful.

I dislike groups of fourteen year-olds walking around in dark hoodies and jeans, holding out a plastic grocery bag while mumbling "Trih' uh Treeh." Listen, kid, I know you're too old for this. You know you're too old for this. We both know I am merely bargaining to not have my house egged but at least pretend this is something besides a holiday-themed shakedown.

But my dislike of Halloween is a mere pothole compared with the Grand Canyon of loathing my cat feels for this idiotic ritual. Of course she doesn't know it, but Halloween is responsible for Lu having one completely miserable week each and every year.

Lulabelle is a black cat. Wherever there are cruel people with time on their hands, animals can get hurt. As Halloween approaches, being a black cat increases the likelihood of mistreatment tenfold. This is so generally understood, most cat-rescue groups will allow someone to adopt a black cat in October, but they cannot take it home until after November first.

Last Friday, when Lulabelle came strolling home from whatever feline mayhem she had subjected the neighborhood to, I explained in a firm yet sympathetic tone, "Did you enjoy yourself out there today, sweetie? I hope so, because it's going to have to hold you until next Tuesday."

She stared indifferently at me for a second then commenced to remove something from between her toes. The next morning, she demanded her breakfast as usual. Then, as usual, she did the feline equivalent of grabbing a travel-cup of coffee and attaché case, stood impatiently by the back door, caught my eye and meowed loudly.

Meanwhile, Polly had also walked to the back door and looked up at me anxiously. Polly's day-planner would have only three entries: Eat. Sleep. Excrete. Many would envy her regularity. But on this spectacular autumn morning the door remained closed. She whined softly.

I arrived at the back door and, in a single motion, grabbed the cat and tossed her towards the kitchen, opened the door and pushed Polly outside before the cat could scramble out. Lulabelle's body, sprinting for freedom, made a solid "thunk" when it connected with the suddenly re-closed door.

Eighty-five seconds later (our Polly is a Swiss watch of bowel predictability) there was a single familiar bark. This time, I grabbed, tossed, opened and pulled Polly back inside while Lulabelle made another sidelong lunge for freedom. Her irritation at missing her shot was assuaged—but only slightly—by sinking her claws into Polly's passing rump.

The week passed. Mostly, Lulabelle hovered near the back door as if it were the last helicopter out of Saigon. I discovered Polly goes out much more than I ever noticed and got to practice the grab-toss-open-push/pull-thunk maneuver at least ten times a day. Without the outside world to supervise, Lulabelle has turned into a soccer hooligan. Polly gets whomped-on regularly and no one's ankles are safe from ambush.

Lulabelle doesn't limit herself to physical violence. This dark warrior has many arrows in her quiver. When she determines none of us are likely to be going out the back door any time soon, she goes to the Bench of Random Objects, locates the lightest-colored sweater, curls up and proceeds to weave her anthracite hair permanently into its warp. Since I have had pets my entire life, I am reasonably vigilant about putting my clothes away, but Consort is now the proud owner of several crew-neck domestic cats. The really neat trick is how this jet-black cat, when confronted with a navy-blue cashmere sport jacket, manages to shed white fur.

"You want me around 24/7?" she thinks as she randomly cross-stitches one-third of her coat into a pair of loden wool pants. "Fine. You can wear me into the next decade."

Temporarily harboring the world's smallest political prisoner also means we now enter the house in an entirely new way. Whenever Lulabelle hears someone approaching any exterior door, she crouches into position, an arrow poised to spring out the merest crack of light. Knowing this is waiting inside the house means one has to be prepared.

Imagine I'm walking with a metal detector, swinging it back and forth in a recognizably ungainly sweep. Now, replace "metal detector" with "foot", and attempt to carry several grocery bags and steer Daughter through door at the same time. What you end up with is a bizarre hopping dance that resembles the traditional jig from a country where people drink a lot and wear uncomfortable shoes.

Throughout this performance, I'm usually shouting for Daughter to "Get in, GET IN!" while simultaneously shouting at the cat, "Stop it, STOP IT!" Usually, Polly comes to see what's going on, so I'm also shouting, "Sit, SIT!"

Of course, what comes out is, "GET SIT! STOP...IN! SIT SET! GOP. STEP! GIT!..."

All three freeze in place for a second, if for no other reason than to observe what happens when an adult human throws an embolism. I exploit this moment of confusion to slam the door closed and shout for Consort to please make me a drink.

So far this week, Lulabelle has breached the perimeter twice, once with Consort and once with me. She dashed outside and, possibly dazzled by daylight, flopped down for a nap only yards from the threshold. We each walked slowly towards her, crooning something like, "What a pretty cat. Come here, pretty girl, and let me pet you." Both times, she allowed herself to be petted, only to wail in distress when we scooped her up and brought her indoors:

LULABELLE: I can't believe I fell for that!

QUINN: Just three more days, sweetie. You're on parole in three more days.

LULABELLE: I feel so stupid.

QUINN: Look, wet food for the prisoner!

LULABELLE: So I see.

QUINN: I'm doing this for your safety, you know.

LULABELLE: Later tonight, I'm going to throw up in your lingerie drawer.

QUINN: It would feel wrong if you didn't.

That night, I realized something mildly disheartening. During the past week I have had a variation of the same conversation with one daughter and two pets, all with varying degrees of success:

QUINN: I know you want to (do cartwheels on the couch)(eat a large rubber band)(live off the land and only come home for wet food) but it's not safe and I can't let you do it. That's my job. I don't enjoy the sound of (an animal crying in pain) (a child crying in pain) (myself crying in pain when I see the Emergency Room bill). So, you will need to find something else to do. End of discussion.

I mean well, but I think they're getting an apartment together. And I don't think any of them are giving me a Christmas present this year.

TURKEY IN THE STRAW

Ah, it's good to be back.

Those of you who are new to these posts, or who don't know me very well, might be thinking, "I wonder if Quinn did something inexplicably stupid during the week she was gone?"

Those of you who do know me are thinking, "I wonder how many of the inexplicably stupid things Quinn did last week will be in the new post?"

Well, for your amusement and edification, I have created a virtual slide show of my misbehavior from the past week. Please turn off the lights and grab a Red Vine or two from the common jar. Get comfortable. Here we go.

(click)

Oh, yeah, this one. Here I am in a suburban neighborhood, gathering twigs and branches and cramming them in the trunk of my car. No, I'm not creating a giant nest on our roof. I am attempting to appease Hephaestus, the God of Fire. My fireplace is a cold, unyielding chamber, capable of extinguishing the driest kindling or the most incendiary starter log with cruel indifference. Nevertheless, through (much) trial and (endless) error, I have determined that the fireplace will produce a reasonably attractive fire if it is fed an endless diet of small sticks. It also seems to like when I sing a Tom Jones song or two.

One problem is that pre-cut fireplace logs come in one size: log. Apparently, other fireplaces like their meals of a reasonable size. Another problem is that I'm cheap. Two weeks ago, we had several days of extremely high winds which neatly denuded many local trees of just the sort of small branches my fireplace craves. And they were free! The only cost was to my dignity.

When driving through peaceful, tree-lined neighborhoods, I have gotten into the habit of parking the car, accumulating armfuls of sticks and putting them in my trunk. Because I am not entirely clear as to the legal definition of trespassing, I try to keep my foraging to the easement—the strip between the sidewalk and the street. However, if the inventory is choice and the street seems deserted then, yes, I *will* head onto someone's lawn and gather up a clump of fat juicy twigs.

To that lady who might have been watching me from her picture window for several minutes as I scampered around your yard obsessively gathering up kindling: I am so sorry for any distress I might have caused you. However, once I spotted you staring out at me, my weird, guilty smile and my wildly gesticulating, "May I have these for my house?" probably calmed your nerves right down. So, thank you for not calling the police. It would have been hard to explain.

(Click)

Here's me again, standing at my front door. Why I am making that strange expression? The strange expression is because I am shouting. What I'm shouting is the embarrassing part, not what I'm wearing — although I would appreciate it if everyone forgets that I'm still wearing *those* pajama bottoms and haven't consigned them to the rag bag.

I've lived with cats my entire life and it is my considered opinion that they come in two variations: cats that would no more eat human food than they would eat human sunglasses; and cats who view any unattended plate as an invitation to devour whatever it offers. Lulabelle falls unrepentantly into the "You gonna cat that?" category.

A while back, Daughter determined that Lulabelle liked soy turkey. What made Daughter first test this hypothesis I will never know; possibly it was the moment she realized the more soy turkey her cat ate, the less she'd have to eat. But by the time Daughter shrieked "Mommy, come SEE this!" from the kitchen, she was leaning over with a small strip of beige dangling from her fingers, and the cat was on her hind legs, stretching precariously to get that precious gobbet of taupe soy goodness.

Over the next few days, we determined that Lulabelle would walk on her hind legs for soy turkey; she would dance for soy turkey; she would finish my taxes for soy turkey. I also noticed that when either Daughter or I said, "Let's get some soy turkey", the cat would race to the fridge. As an experiment I tried just saying "Soy" and I tried just saying "Turkey" but in either case, the cat regally ignored me and continued to groom her sphincter. It had to be the whole phrase, "Soy turkey", preferably spoken in an excited *Whee! Isn't someone the luckiest cat in the world!* tone of voice.

To be specific, I would start the word "Soy" in the mid-range, gain an octave on the "O", settle tenuously at the top of my singing range for the "Y", skip upwards for a breathtaking second for "Tur-", and come down again into the mezzo-soprano category for "-key!"

This way, the cat gets the double pleasure of anticipating a yummy, faux meat product and watching me behave like an absolute nutjob.

We've had evening coyote sightings in the neighborhood lately so Lulabelle gets to spend, at most, her mornings outside. She spends her afternoons and evenings inside, planning escape routes. Last night, when I went out the front door to check whether the sprinklers went on, she nimbly slithered under one leg, vaulted the next, and darted into the darkness. I shrieked and grabbed after her, but was rewarded with a single black hair stuck to my index finger, a mocking memento of the *Cat Who Would Not Be Taken Alive.*

I waited a few minutes by the open door but she remained hidden in the shadows. I chirruped, which sometimes brings her running, but was rewarded with silence. Actually, double silence — the sprinklers hadn't turned on either. Double silence equals double exasperation. *Something* had to be remedied this evening and it probably wasn't going to be the irrigation system.

I took a deep breath.

"SOY *TUR*-KEY!"

Still silence, but somehow it felt more...attentive. She was under a nearby bush, I could *feel* it.

"SOY *TUR*-KEY!"

Still nothing, although I was happy to note my neighbors weren't yelling for me to shut the hell up. Then again, it might have been fun if they started yelling random foodstuffs. Maybe the couple next door could holler "Condensed Milk!" followed by the elderly woman on the other side chiming in with "Peas and Carrots!" Then everyone could come over to my yard and ask why I've been stealing sticks from their lawns.

But where was the cat? Oh, wait. I needed ammunition. I walked to the kitchen and peeled off some of the genuine article. If you live the kind of life that doesn't involve soy turkey and need a visual, imagine a thin, flat circle of Silly Putty which, I think, also pretty accurately describes its taste. I walked back to the front door and dangled temptation just inside the threshold.

"SOY *TUR*-KEY!"

Lulabelle moved so quickly I felt the breeze of her passing and the tug of soy turkey being yanked from my fingers before I actually registered her presence. She dragged the soy turkey to the corner of the living room and killed it in quiet triumph.

I closed the door and sat nearby on the floor, counting my fire sticks.

MY GUY

I spend a lot of my time here making fun of Consort. This is because I can. This is also because Consort has the style to think most of the snarky things I write about him are funny. I understand he frequently directs friends to the posts that itemize his more dramatic foibles in 12-point font. Also, I fear the grand romantic gesture. I grew up in Los Angeles, a place where if couples are loudly proclaiming their love in public, the publicity release announcing their separation is about a week away.

But I am going to risk it all and tell you two ways in which Consort, quite simply, has rocked recently.

First, he continues to live with me and that's not a small thing. Consort is an easy-going, gregarious man who enjoys the company of friends. I am a person who reads about executions and pandemics for pleasure and enjoys the company of other like-minded individuals, should I ever meet one. But that speaks to his baseline awesomeness. This week, he iced the cake.

Daughter and I had arrived at the animal rescue place where we volunteer, to manage the afternoon feed and litter-box restoration. Since we are the only people who work Friday afternoons, you might imagine my surprise when I found two people back in the isolation area. The rescue organization shares space with a pet store and they had simply walked in, past several bold "personnel only" signs, and took it upon themselves to get to know the cats. Most disturbing, one of these interlopers had reached into a cage housing a mother cat that had given birth just five days before, and was picking through the litter. I semi-politely kicked them both out and called the woman who runs the rescue group. It was decided that the mother cat and her kittens needed to be someplace quiet and safe, someplace off-site.

Okay, now imagine you are at my house three minutes later. The phone is ringing. Consort picks it up.

CONSORT: Hello?

QUINN: Hi, it's me. Listen, I have a favor to ask. Can you create a space about, oh, four feet square on the workbench in the garage?

CONSORT: Sure.

(Silence)

CONSORT: Why?

QUINN: Um, we're going to have houseguests.

(Silence)

CONSORT: How many?

QUINN: Eleven.

At this point, Consort would have had many conversational options at his disposal. He could have gone with "For how long?" or "Why?" or "I'm moving someplace where things like this don't happen and please forward my mail to Kate Beckinsale's house," but he didn't—even though it would have been completely within his rights.

You see, this happens a lot, and he knew nothing of this when we fell in love. Quinn, the somewhat cute, somewhat affable vegetarian of our first date is also Quinn, the woman who keeps an emergency leash in her glove compartment in case she sees a stray dog. Consort—who over the entire course of his life had taken care of a dog for exactly two weeks and also has a profound loathing of lint—has gracefully accepted all of it.

So, we now have a sweet mom-cat and ten kittens living in a spacious crate in our garage. The mother specializes in eating and nursing. She also purrs a lot, possibly in gratitude for a lack of strange hands mauling her babies, possibly in hopes of eliciting more chow. The babies specialize in having tiny pansy faces, practice opening and closing their eyes and try to nurse off each other's ears. Half the time, I check in on them; half the time, Consort does. I apologize to him, often, for making his life less *House Beautiful* and more *Animal Planet.* He smiles and says, "I wouldn't have it any other way," and I am filled with such love that I refrain from describing the wonderful article I just read about the symptomatic manifestations of the Flu epidemic of 1917.

RABBIT RUN

One afternoon last month, Daughter and I were taking a stroll around the neighborhood. Half-listening to a baroque, lengthy and mind-numbingly detailed account of lunch-table melodrama, my eye was pulled to a subtle movement under a nearby hedge.

Cat, I thought. Black cat. Hopping under plant.

I took another step and tried to focus on Daughter's endless saga about who sits next to whom and why, but my brain disobediently looped back to the sighting.

Cats don't hop.

I retraced my steps and looked under the shrubbery. Something stared back.

Cats also don't have long floppy ears and chew sticks.

"Look," I said intelligently to Daughter. "A rabbit!"

She squealed in delight and flung herself on the ground to gaze adoringly at the rabbit. The rabbit, understandably, viewed sudden movement and a loud piercing squeal as something a hungry predator might do and took off past the driveway, up through an open gate.

Daughter's jutting lower lip told me an impending three-block lecture about how I had scared away the rabbit (whom she was going to adopt and call 'Bootsy') was going to be censorious, richly detailed, and make me yearn for the seating-arrangement saga. At that moment, however, the Fates smiled upon me. Hopping through the open gate was another rabbit. This one was a wee little thing, white, with ears nearly as long as its body.

"Look," I noted. "Another rabbit!"

[I reserve my linguistic flourishes for times when I'm not trying to keep my child from whining.]

Again, the squealing in delight. Again, the flinging. Again, the darting away. This time, however, Daughter didn't have time to draw her eyebrows together before yet another rabbit (mid-size, black and white, one straight ear, one lop-ear) appeared from the yard next door and headed towards the gate.

Daughter cooed and stalked the third rabbit as I considered this situation. I'm not always the first person to pick up on trends but seeing three rabbits in two minutes, all of whom seemed to have an awareness of this house and its open back gate, signaled something in my minimally active brainstem. I looked more closely at the house. In a neighborhood where lots of people are doing lots of home-improvement, this one stubbornly clung to its "before" status. I walked past the car up on cinderblocks and approached a front door wallpapered in pizza delivery flyers. I knocked. I rang what appeared to be a broken doorbell. I yodeled a few "Hellooooo?"s. Nothing.

Just as I was turning to leave, three boys slouched up the driveway. They all sported the same teenage Emo haircut that leaves, at most, part of one's chin and a sliver of ear exposed. I smiled brightly at the hair mushroom nearest me who, as indicated by the appearance of a house key, appeared to live there.

"Hi! Are these your rabbits?" I asked, gesturing towards the rabbits, which were being lovingly stalked by Daughter. I noticed three more had joined the party.

The key-wielding hair mushroom stood rock still. He was at the magic age when direct questions from adults, especially female adults, dry up the throat and stifle the ability to answer even yes-or-no questions. I knew this, but he was the closest thing I had to a source of information. I repeated, slowly, gesturing like Vanna White, "ARE. THESE. (Swinging hand gesture over furry doorstops) YOUR. RABBITS?"

His head turned and the hair split enough so one eye was briefly exposed. He squinted at this surge of daylight and goggled at the rabbits. His friends stared at their shoes. One hummed. A minute passed.

He finally got out, "Yeah."

I was about to offer to help move them back into their cages when all of sudden, he got chatty.

"We breed rabbits. For pets. Or food. Whatever. Anyway. You can buy a rabbit. For a pet. Or, you know. Food. You want to buy a rabbit?"

I thought this degree of salesmanship was adorable, if misguided, considering that four more inventory units had fled through the back gate while he was making his pitch.

"Thanks," I said gently, trying to herd a couple more who were heading down the walkway. "I'll certainly think about it. But, in the meanwhile, you might want to...catch them and lock them up?"

The clumps of hair looked at one another, to the degree objects lacking eyeballs can be said to look at anything. Clearly, the afternoon's plans of huffing paint and watching *Beverly Hillbillies* re-runs might be compromised by this new project.

Silence.

The alpha hair mushroom said, "Yeah."

I had no idea what he just agreed to, or with. I'm not sure he did either, but it gave a certain anemic closure to the whole discussion. They went inside. I corralled Daughter and we continued on our stroll.

Do I have to tell you how this is playing out?

Already, don't you instinctively know that no one in that house bothered to wrangle the herd, which means we now have a population of rabbits free-ranging for several blocks in every direction?

Need I explain that the latest nighttime driving hazard in our neighborhood is two rabbits in the middle of the street, urgently making more of themselves?

Would you like to know how many neighborhood dog owners have dislocated shoulders from their leashed dog's leaping like stallions after a rabbit that has waited cunningly under a shrub until the dog is just close enough to care?

Do you care that the city told me that even if I were to catch some of them, they don't have room for any more rabbits in the shelters?

On the plus side, the day before Easter found Daughter and I heading off to an errand when, crossing through the front yard, she spotted movement under the lavender bush.

"MOMMY, LOOK!" she chirped. "It's the EASTER BUNNY!"

Yes, sweetheart. It's also the other white meat.

PUT THEM ALL TOGETHER THEY SPELL "MOTHER"

For those who have written in to ask: "Yes, Quinn. But when are you going to write about how you've taken responsibility for these drive-by rabbits?" let me assure you, it won't be happening.

Please don't snicker.

No, I really can't take on rabbit rescue. I'm not saying I haven't left out elderly, rubbery carrots for a large and especially phlegmatic buck currently dwelling under the roses but neither that rabbit nor any other will be coming into my house. For one thing, I am wildly allergic to rabbits. Should one fingertip tentatively pet soft rabbit fur and then touch my face at any point over the next six hours then, lo and behold, my skull will puff up to seventy-five times its natural volume. My head battling one such histamine overdose was seen bobbing down Broadway last Thanksgiving morning, right behind Hello Kitty.

Another reason I will never be a rabbit owner: they chew electrical cords. We are the kind of desperate, geeky people who start rocking and moaning if our online connection is compromised. I don't care how precious your l'il lop ears are; if you impede my ability to browse gossip websites I'll reconsider my vegetarian status.

But the most significant reason we will not be having extra pets in this household any time soon is because, after six weeks, we still have eleven cats living in our garage. It's hard to even imagine even one more houseguest when we have an entire feline youth hostel sharing towels and nipples on Consort's workbench. Our little boarders are a comic opera of saucer eyes, darling fat tummies, fluffy pipe-clearer tails and a degree of aggression towards their littermates that would make Cain wince. But the real hero in this story is the mother cat who, had I been better organized, would have gotten her own blog entry on Mother's Day.

We called her "Cat" for the first week. Yes, it's a little generic but considering how any statement referencing her ran along the lines of "Put the food closer to Cat's head; the kittens won't stop nursing long enough for her to get at her food", I doubt she was terribly offended.

The following weekend, I was at the rescue facility ordering supplies when I met the volunteer who first brought her in. It seems momma cat had been living behind a block of subsidized housing units in an extremely chaotic neighborhood of Los Angeles when the rescue worker, an elementary-school teacher, was alerted by one of her students that a highly pregnant cat was staging a delivery room under some scraggy brush near a bus stop. She swung by the bus stop that afternoon, dropped Cat into a cardboard box and brought her straight to the rescue shelter. I assured this sweet woman that "her" cat was doing well.

"Does she have a name?" I asked while counting cans of food. The woman's pale skin sprouted a little blush.

"I didn't pick her name. The neighbors who had been feeding her named her."

I paused between Tuna Terrific and Turkey Treaties and looked at her, eyebrows up.

"So she does have a name?"

The woman looked around, leaned in towards me and whispered, "La Juana."

I stared off for a second and then composed myself.

"So, if you wanted to be completely accurate, you might say she's La Juana, the struggling single mother of ten who lives in subsidized housing?"

She nodded. We gazed at one another.

I asked tentatively, "You don't suppose anyone would mind if we...?"

"Changed her name? I think that would be a..."

"...wonderful idea!" we chorused together.

Because I don't need anyone thinking this is my achingly bad attempt at keeping it real.

Her name is now Charlotte, after the spider, because she is a very good mother with a noble soul and we should never confuse nobility with weakness. I got some sense of how deeply her maternal instincts ran after we had been keeping her safe for about two weeks. I was spending time in the garage with her and the kittens one morning when our dog loped casually into the back yard. Polly genuinely loves cats and, no, not as an entrée. In fact, the sight of a cat makes Polly shimmy in pure joy but it's the rare cat who feels likewise. Unbeknownst to me, the side door into the garage wasn't completely closed. Polly used the initiative she usually reserves for eating the inedible to wedge open the door with her nose, so she might finally bask in the feline essence she had been hearing and smelling within for so many days.

Polly stood in the doorway for a second. I rose up to my feet to shut the door but Charlotte was faster than I was. Much faster. Polly was a pathetic portrait of misguided hope, tail wagging, a warm pleased expression on her face. Charlotte leapt neatly onto that expression, sunk her claws into the dog's head, and commenced to beat her skull with the precise brutality of a gang initiation. It took no more than thirty seconds for Polly to flee the garage, half of which was spent trying to disengage cat nails from her eyeballs. Task accomplished, Charlotte sauntered back to her cage, checked on the kittens, and finished grooming her back leg.

As I learned more about Charlotte's life as La Juana, my understanding and respect for her grew. According to the rescuer, who had talked to her students on site, La Juana was about three years old. She had spent her entire life living under the hedge where she was found, producing litter after litter. And every time, she would lose at least half of each litter to neighborhood dogs. One night, the father of one student heard something outside the bedroom window and shone a flashlight into the alley. There was Charlotte/La Juana, stationed between her kittens and two feral dogs, making the most god-awful sound an eight-pound cat has ever made. The dogs considered a delicious treat of kitten McNuggets weighed against this maternal ninja assassin and decided it wasn't worth it. They walked off. Another cat was found dead in the yard the next morning but La Juana saved her kittens for another day. I feel a certain sympathy for Polly, but Charlotte has earned to right to think any dog she meets deserves a lesson in trepanning.

I won't go into every story I heard about Charlotte's previous life. Suffice to say, this is an exceptionally nice cat who has been the hero in her own adventure far too often. It is possible, however, her luck might finally have turned. In four days, her kittens will be mature enough to go to their new homes. She has, I keep promising her, done her last heavy lifting; she purrs and kneads when I say that.

On this night after Mother's Day, as her kittens lie in a warm lump, snoring and chewing on one another safely in their cage as they sleep, Charlotte is recovering at a local pet hospital after a long-overdue spaying.

I have promised her we will find her a loving, dog-free home and a long, uneventful life of sunny windowsills, choice fish bits, and a family to call her own.

QUINN CUMMINGS

A CAT'S ENTITLED TO EXPECT / THESE EVIDENCES OF RESPECT

Sorry for the delay in writing. The system was down.

And by "system", I mean "Quinn".

And by "down", I mean "eating her weight in Peeps".

It's hard to write after eating one's weight in Peeps. For one thing, your fingers are sticky. For another, you're shaking and sobbing and keening for French fries to offset the sugar. Also, you end up staying awake for three days solid, writing a 17,000-word manifesto on how much you despise mayonnaise. You then insist to your life partner that this would make a marvelous light opera.

Anyway...

So, what's new with me? Well, we still have the Cat Family. At the end of the week, the kittens will move to a new foster home where there is an entire room dedicated to their ambulation. Right now, they still live in a pile in a blanket-lined box within the larger cage. Last Wednesday, one of the kittens figured out that pushing a smaller sibling off a nipple and appropriating that nipple was highly effective. The rest of the litter quickly took the cue and began duking it out, all except the smallest. By the end of the day, Charlotte's abdomen was a rippling wave of paw-swipes, head-butts and body slams—the Ultimate Nursing Challenge—with one wee little kitten standing on Madame Cat's head and wailing.

Not surprisingly, Charlotte has begun to look a bit imprisoned. Every time one of us would go in the garage to feed her, check her water or just get in the car and leave, she would lean against the cage door and *stare at us*. My Spanish is embarrassing and my French laughable, but I speak Mother across the species divide:

"Please, I'm begging you! I need a few minutes where someone isn't hanging from my nipple or trying to nurse from my ear."

I sympathized. Hell, I even empathized. But I just couldn't let her out, even in the confines of the garage.

I worried she would find some small hole in the garage wall and make a break for freedom.

I worried she would find a puddle of anti-freeze on the ground, drink it and die, and then I would be responsible for bottle-feeding ten kittens with endless appetites and a penchant for kung fu.

I worried she would bring sawdust back into the cage, and the kittens would come down with the feline, wood-based equivalent of silicosis.

Mostly, I worried I was going to screw up fostering her if I let her out of the cage and despite my willingness to air all my screw-ups in my writing, I don't actually like screwing up. So, I would scratch her head sympathetically and block her exit as I spooned more food into her saucer.

Consort, however, is made of kinder stuff. Not being able to account for him one evening, I went out to the garage. He was standing next to the cage admiring the vari-colored mass of writhing fur. On the floor of the garage was Charlotte. I slammed the side door shut quickly, so she couldn't fly past me.

QUINN: I thought we weren't going to let her out.

CONSORT: I came out to feed her, and when I opened the door she basically jumped over my shoulder and down to the ground. She walked around for a few minutes.

QUINN: And then what?

Consort looked over at her.

CONSORT: She did *that.*

I watched her a moment. She was lying on the ground, looking around. She wasn't eating anything toxic; she wasn't trying to claw her way through the back door. Cats don't have a wide range of expression but this was something approaching perfect contentment. She was me on my first errand away from home when Daughter was six weeks old: *my offspring is safe, I will go back to work as soon as I am really needed but right now, not doing anything feels like a week in Tahiti.*

I sat on the garage floor, scratched Charlotte's head and told her what a good mom she was. I offered to bring her a margarita and the *Four Weddings and a Funeral* DVD. I mean, if she's going to have a real evening off from the kids...

That very day, the kittens learned you don't need to abuse your littermates for nipple dominance alone; it's also highly pleasurable to use one's newly sprouted, razor-sharp baby teeth to simply make another living thing cry. Throughout my stay in the garage, there had been a series of bleats and howls from the cage. Charlotte didn't so much as flick an ear towards Consort or her litter. This indicated both her trust in Consort's baby-sitting abilities and a deeply felt need to pretend she was still Carrie Bradshaw and not Ma Walton. The noise, however, began to increase in both volume and anxiety. Without having raised feline dectuplets myself, it was still easy to guess they were getting hungry again and low-blood sugar was causing them to gnaw each other with renewed vigor.

Charlotte emitted the tiniest sigh of feline resignation, got up slowly, stretched every muscle and ligament which probably hadn't been moved since the night she met the handsome tabby who got her into all this trouble, and headed back to the cage. She brushed by Consort, who closed the cage door behind her, and delicately stepped into the box with her kittens who, upon sight of the Spigot Goddess, created a sound like ten tiny car alarms. She lay down and the kittens pounced, taking any opportunity to inflict harm on a sibling while getting settled in for dinner.

Every day since, either Consort or I have pulled the car out of the garage, made sure all the doors and windows were shut, and let Charlotte walk around. Sometimes, I slide away from my own chores and sit on a folding chair reading a fashion magazine while she grooms herself and stares off into space. Before a half-hour has passed, one of the children—hers or mine—is demanding a maternal intervention of some sort.

We bid polite adieus and promise to have another get-together as soon as our schedules permit.

YOU GOTTA BE CRAZY, YOU GOTTA HAVE A REAL NEED

Many years ago, before Daughter was even a glint in the eye of a *My Little Pony* retailer, a friend told me a story of coming home from the hospital with her brand-new son.

They stepped carefully into their 900 square-foot Park Slope apartment and my friend decided to sit on the couch with her new baby while her husband moved in the 400 square feet of presents their tiny boy had accumulated in the twenty-four hours since being born. As she sat there gazing rapturously at her son, their cat jumped on the couch and stared balefully at her, in that way much-loved cats do when you've been gone two days and they discover an intruder in what they've assumed to be *their* lap.

"Wow," thought my friend. "Katrina's a *cat.*"

When I first heard this story, I'm sure I thought something like "Well, *yes.* The meowing might have been your first clue."

But she was right — and I was just being a big snotty snot-box of know-nothingness. What, before parenthood, is a darling near-child without the burdens of hygiene and school tuition becomes, after parenthood...a pet. A beloved pet, for certain. Perhaps even a well-regarded housemate with a healthier, more regular diet and better social habits than most roommates, but still an animal. I'm not sure I'd want to see the dynamics in a family where the beloved pet demanded back its original rank and privilege once the baby arrives.

My parents had a dog when I showed up: a coyote/German Shepherd-mix named Ginger. Some people might consider a dog of that combination playing with a human baby to be a dog playing with its food but, in this case, they would be wrong. Ginger gave up her position as *Alpha Baby* without a peep because I—the new alpha baby—introduced a far more thrilling challenge to any dog with shepherding blood: I was a *job*. Working breeds, like German Shepherds, need things to *do*. Otherwise they make their own fun, which usually involves your most expensive shoes testing the efficacy of their teeth. To her way of thinking, Ginger was given the job of a lifetime.

I would squeak in the bassinet and Ginger would run and get my mother, barking and nosing her until she checked in on me.

I would cry and Ginger's greatest agitation seemed to be that she couldn't develop opposable thumbs fast enough to change my diaper or bandage my knee.

As I grew, Ginger developed all the talents a small girl could dream of. She would eat whatever vile vegetable I slipped under the table. She wore any outfit I put on her. She would sleep next to me every night, no matter how hard it was for her to climb up onto the bed as she grew older and the arthritis set in. I was fourteen when she died and I cried for days, as much for this irrevocable milestone of my youth as the not-surprising death of a very old dog.

But that's what pets are, or more accurately, what they *do*. They become as much a reflection of who you are at certain times in your life as they are a manifestation of their own innate personalities. Think back to my friend, her newborn, and her cat. Did the cat change in the two days she and her husband went to the hospital? Doubtful, unless you count the hairball she left in an unexpected place as a message of her displeasure with the babysitter.

My friend changed, so her relationship with the cat changed, so the cat was changed. Something tells me this cat wasn't getting her tuna nuked for exactly eight seconds every night at 6:30 to take the chill off. Not any more. Something tells me the cat somehow survived this.

Polly entered our lives when Daughter was six months old. Consort had gone out of town on a trip that was part business, part pleasure. Skiing was involved. This was to be my first week alone with Daughter. Just us. Consort asked, repeatedly, if we were going to be okay without him and insisted he could reschedule his trip. I believe I actually scoffed.

"I lived by myself for years. YEARS! The child will be fine. The house will be fine. And I will be fine."

The child *was* fine. The house was fine. Turns out, I was *not* fine. Turns out, the house makes all sorts of noises every single night which sound exactly like someone breaking in to surprise the mother and child trapped inside and harm them in unspeakable ways. Sometimes, the house would make noises that sounded like someone disabling the alarm system before breaking in to do unspeakable things. I believe I slept no more than ten minutes at a stretch the entire time he was gone.

I desperately wanted a dog to protect us when Consort was out of town. Worst-case scenario: if the dog's barking didn't ward off homicidal maniacs, I could at least throw the dog at any intruder, giving Daughter and I time to escape through a window or something while the maniac and the dog went at it. Since I wasn't aware of a company that rented maniac-repelling dogs on a temporary basis, I was going to have to acquire a full-time dog. Also, Daughter liked dogs. She squealed with joy when one licked her toes. Of course, she also squealed with joy when they replaced the tape in the grocery-store register. Life is a medley of spontaneous entertainment for the twelve-months-and-under crowd.

Every day he was gone, Consort would call at least twice a day. For the first three days, I kept up a brave front. But by day four, I was exhausted, cunning, and looking to close the deal. Clearly, Consort had no idea we were negotiating...

(PHONE RINGS)

QUINN: ...Hello?

CONSORT: Hey, it's me! You sound tired. Did she sleep well last night?

QUINN: Oh, *she* slept fine.

CONSORT: But you didn't?

QUINN: I'm fine. So, remember how you asked me if there was anything you could bring back from your trip?

CONSORT: Yes...?

QUINN: I have a gift idea. And it won't cost you anything.

CONSORT: Go on...

This last should be read in a halting and suspicious voice.

QUINN: We get rid of the television. As I have suggested many times already. You basically use it like talking wallpaper. It's a huge time-suck. And it will force our daughter to worship Elmo.

A horrified silence from the away-side of the conversation. After a good moment to let it sink in fully...

QUINN: (in an upbeat tone) Or...

CONSORT: Or?...

QUINN: We get a dog.

A beat.

CONSORT: What kind of dog?

Yes, readers. It went like that.

Consort got home Friday night. We were at the shelter first thing Saturday morning. As far as he knew, this was an exploratory trip only. As far as he knew, he had all the dog-free time in the world. I knew he was traveling again in three weeks and desperately wanted a barking sentry in place before then.

I might have implied this was my first trip to the shelter, which might have been belied by the unswerving path we followed towards one particular cage in one particular area of the shelter; or by the number of staffers who said "Oh, hello Quinn. Back again?"

Her name was Polly, and she while she wasn't the last dog I would have picked at the shelter, she was certainly in the bottom ten. I had taken Daughter to the shelter the previous day to do a little reconnaissance and pre-audition a dog to show Consort. I imagined a cheerful, eternally smiling mutt of such raffish ancestry the only sure bet would be that at least one parent had been some kind of dog.

Let me tell you a little bit about this shelter. If you are a dog or cat alone in this world, you pray to be picked up by these people. It's a no-kill shelter with shaded outdoor kennels and an architectural warmth throughout. In the summer, staffers mist the floors of the kennels for comfort. And there's no such thing as impetuous pet-adopting here. Before meeting any dog, you are required to fill out an application detailing your previous pet experience, current housing situation, expectations for this pet, and so on. I wish someone had put me through a similar filter before I picked certain boyfriends.

I finished my written application and explained to the volunteer that I had a six month-old bundle of love, gesturing towards the car seat and my daughter, at this moment mesmerized by an enclosure full of chickens. I was living a pretty densely packed life. I wanted an easy, un-dramatic, adult dog that wouldn't bother our cat. The volunteer said thoughtfully, "I think Polly's the right dog for you."

If one can be said to skip while carrying an infant car seat, I fairly skipped behind this woman through the kennel. We passed darling Lab puppies with paws like furry saucers; exuberant small dogs prancing in circles desperate for our attention; seasoned older dogs pushing their noses at the bars hoping for a scratch. What wondrous dog had she planned for us?

We got to the last cage in the section. On the ground, lying curled up in a ball, was a dog of a certain age. Not just a dog but a purebred Dalmatian; a species known for freakish amounts of energy and very little sense. This one, however, looked more like an area rug.

The volunteer called, "Polly?" and was rewarded with a sigh.

A depressed area rug.

The volunteer unlocked the cage and Polly looked up. Once she realized she had visitors she got to her feet, her entire body exuding indifference. The volunteer snapped on a leash to take all of us to the Family Meeting Area and explained a bit of Polly's story as we walked. She was somewhere between four and six and had been owned by an elderly person who died. Her owner's relatives brought her in on New Year's Day. This was February first.

"She's been here a month?"

"Yeah. She doesn't show very well."

This was putting it mildly. I sat down on the bench in the meeting area. Polly stood in the corner, staring at the ground. When called by name, she walked over and gazed up at me neutrally. Her entire body fairly sang "You'll forgive me, but I've done this about a hundred times already, and you're not going to adopt me, so I don't really feel like faking it. Also, I just want to go home."

The volunteer scratched her ears and said worriedly, "She's a lovely girl. She just misses her owner so much; no one gets to see how sweet she is. She loves cats. She gets along with everyone. She's crate-trained and house-broken and she's been here so long..."

Polly sighed and put her head on the bench next to my leg, and slowly, I started to feel the most dangerous and ill-advised of all of my emotional states:

I can fix this one.

Which is how Consort and I ended up at the shelter the next day, looking down at a depressed, spotted area rug being snapped onto a leash. If she remembered me at all, it wasn't lifting her mood any.

Our first meeting as a family didn't exactly inspire "*Your best friend can be found at your local shelter*" anecdotes. I threw a ball. Polly stared at it and sighed. Consort called her name. She feigned deafness. But there were moments. Unbidden, Polly came up to me and sniffed at Daughter in my lap. Consort scratched the back of her neck and she leaned against him. For one shining second, she played with a bug she found under a plant. There was a dog in there and it was a dog with another emotion besides terrible sadness.

I looked up from Daughter and Polly, and looked hard at Consort. He was dazed, and it wasn't just jet lag. I took pity on him and suggested we leave for an hour or so; maybe go get some lunch and talk it through.

Polly was walked back to her kennel. As we walked away, I glanced back over my shoulder. Before she fell into her usual stupor, her eyes followed us down the corridor.

At the restaurant, we talked about everything *but* Polly and I started to feel terrible guilt. Consort didn't *want* a dog. If Consort had *wanted* a dog in his life, he would have *had* one and he had never chosen to include a dog in his world for his entire adult life. I didn't need a guard dog. I could sleep with a big Maglite under the pillow when he was out of town. I didn't *need* another pet. I just *wanted* one. And Consort loved me enough to want whatever I wanted that badly.

"Honey," I said without preamble, "let's not get a dog right now. She seems sweet but we've got a cat and an infant and it's enough."

If he looked even slightly relieved, I would let him off the hook.

He looked startled.

"But...Who else is going to take care of our dog?"

It turns out; I am not the only one in this house who hears the siren call of *I can fix this one.*

Polly has been with us for several years. She knows us and I think she likes us, but I am not entirely certain she loves us. I think she had room for one person in her spotted heart and it was the person who died that winter we met. Based upon the disproportionate joy she's always taken from my mother's presence, I suspect it was an older woman. In our loud and complicated household Polly maintains the politely baffled demeanor of a foreign exchange student with no working knowledge of the host's language or culture.

For the first time in my life, I view the pet in my house as an animal and not a family member. Which comes back to where I started: a pet is as much a reflection of you at the time of the pet's life as it is the pet's personality. Polly came into a house where I already had a small person whom I adored and who needed constant care. And we are all okay with this.

Which isn't to say we have slacked in our responsibilities. Polly's shots have been keep current; her teeth are pretty much intact; and when she chose to eat an entire stomach's worth of indigestible plant material or get bitten by a rattlesnake, we ran her to the veterinary ER and paid the enormous bills as they arrived.

But she's growing old. And I realize I'm looking at the end of her life with less of the stress I've typically experienced over losing a pet. We will make sure she lives comfortably, and when that comfort isn't there any more we will make the only kind choice. And on that day I will whisper to her about the winter afternoon we took her to Montecito and let her run wild on the beach where dogs are allowed. She spent all day chasing seagulls with a glee that was matched only by the seagulls' joy in avoiding her. She was beautiful that day. Fast and free. A black-and-white blur running for hours like a racehorse in the sugary dunes. Like the thoroughbred she was. Like a dream.

I will whisper to her of that day while she shuts her eyes, and I will hope she knows I loved her, if not as much as I have loved some dogs, but as much as I was capable of loving any dog right now. And I will hope that was enough.

ALL CREATURES GREAT
AND SMALL

"Quinn, how many animals do you have?"

Wouldn't you think the answer to this question would be a no-brainer? As long as I didn't go for the cheap ...*you mean besides the two who walk upright and get mail at my house, har, har?* joke, it should require a very basic response: a simple numeral, a finger-tip calculation, a whole number on the smallish side. But not for me. Instead, I get the cagy expression of a person being deposed and respond with something like, "What do you mean by *have?*"

"Well, how many do you own?"

Yeah, you're going to have to be more specific than that. Do you mean how many animals are currently living in my house? Or how many animals do I feed? Or do you mean how many animals would I have to evacuate in the unlikely event a hurricane hits the West Coast? Each one of those queries would require a different answer.

If you are asking how many animals currently dwell under my actual roof, then the answer is two. Or three, depending on whether you count our non-attached garage as "under my roof." The tiny foster kittens have grown, attended various adoption events and gone off to live with wonderful, loving families, many of whom soon will be considering reupholstering their furniture. Charlotte, the mother, is a horse of a considerably more challenging color.

Whereas her offspring were all big eyes and wee little paws slipping through the cage bars begging adorably for attention, Charlotte views an adoption fair as some cruel variant of speed-dating. She wants no part of it. She's a healthy, pretty tabby, more than happy to socialize amiably with people who walk by our front yard when she's outside during her supervised sunbathing time. But drag her to an adoption fair on any Saturday morning and she sticks her head under a blanket and refuses to acknowledge anyone until I pick her up Sunday night. The entire time, instead of charming potential domestic hosts, she exudes a palpable cloud of resentment in and around her cage. Unless someone is in the market for a cat that resembles a fourteen year-old girl being forced to attend a family reunion, she's not finding a new home anytime soon.

The remaining five days a week she does not live inside our house because she has terrorized both our cat and our dog—or as we like to think of them: the "preexisting conditions." Polly is an elderly dog. Like many older folk, she needs a bathroom arrangement based upon ease and convenience. By the time she manages to stand on all fours, hobble to the back door and bark, we all know she needs to *get out there now*. However, if I open the door and Charlotte happens to be anywhere in the back yard, Polly turns around and hobbles back to her bed:

POLLY (Sadly): Oh, never mind. I'll urinate another time.

QUINN: What are you doing, you have to go out!

I grab her by the collar and try to drag her outdoors. She splays her legs and goes limp.

POLLY: Oh, I'm fine. Maybe we could put in a catheter or something?

QUINN: CHARLOTTE, GET OUT OF THE YARD!

CHARLOTTE: What? I'm just sitting here. I always sharpen my claws this time of day.

I tug the dog outdoors and grab for the cat. The cat easily avoids my oafish lunge and makes for the dog.

POLLY: AUGH! MY EYES!

As far as our family cat goes, Charlotte appears to have taken stock of Lulabelle and decided she likes Lulabelle's life very much; so much so, in fact, that she would like to live that life, if only Lulabelle weren't selfishly insisting on living it herself. Unless closely monitored, Charlotte runs Lu off the property every day and tries to slip inside the house and sleep in Lu's favorite spots. It's become *Single White Furball*.

Every evening, I go outside and collect Charlotte with a seductive little shake of the dry cat-food container and a lilting refrain. "Kitty stars! Who wants kitty stars?"

Once tucked under my arm, I take her into the garage, give her fresh water and bid her a fond goodnight, closing the door behind me. I then spend the next hour or so cajoling Lu down from the roof, where she's been perched like a baleful, furry gargoyle, berating me for defiling her estate with such an odious trespasser.

"OK", you say. "You have two animals and are fostering another one. You have three animals. Kind of."

Kind of, but not really. Do you recall the rabbits in my neighborhood? Animal Control was called in to address the situation at the breeding house. They showed up eventually and removed the backyard rabbits, but by that point at least a few had made a break for bunny freedom. Within a few days, I became aware of a black rabbit living in my front yard under an overgrown hedge. It was very skinny and it wouldn't let me get anywhere near it. Still, the outside temperature has drifted over a hundred degrees several times this summer so I started leaving out a fresh bowl of water each morning. My friend Amanda, learning of my gatecrasher, kindly offered up some rabbit food left over from a pet who'd gone MIA.

But, see, this isn't pet ownership because I hadn't actually bought the food, right?

Also, rabbit fur sends me right into anaphylactic shock, so it's not coming inside, ever. So it's not my pet, right?

After a week or so, I was heartened to notice the rabbit gaining some weight. Also, sometimes, it would hop towards me in an inquisitive way, which pleased me. I wasn't going to touch the histamine-laden beast, you understand, but a friendlier animal struck me as a happier animal. It was kind of confusing, though. Sometimes, the rabbit would look plump. Sometimes it looked peaked. Sometimes it was quite happy to eat near me. Other times, it would regard me as if I were brandishing a cleaver. I couldn't figure out what was going on with this rabbit.

You're smart. You've already deduced there was more than one rabbit. I didn't get it until I came out one night to leave lettuce tops and saw four of them out there, all black.

I also saw a skunk waddling up to partake of the rabbit food (which I was by now buying by the sack), but under no circumstance am I counting it as one of my animals in any way, shape or form.

After long deliberation, I came to several conclusions:

1) The shelters are full to bursting with rabbits, many of which came from my very neighborhood. No one wants these guys, so...

2) I will keep feeding them and giving them fresh water. I will make their lives as pleasant as possible without actually touching them, and...

3) Since the odds of them being all the same gender were very small, and since I didn't want a rippling, black, furry yard of leporine dependents, I was going to have to get them spayed or neutered. Because we live in a large

city, it will be easy and painless to find a low-cost spaying and neutering program for rabbits. I suspected the greatest challenge of the whole "Getting them neutered" situation was going to be getting them in cages without actually touching them.

[CUE SFX: the Gods who monitor my particular life can be heard hooting in raucous laughter.]

As it turns out, there is no low-cost spaying and neutering program for rabbits in Los Angeles County.

As it turns out, it costs more to spay and neuter a five-pound rabbit than it does an eighty-pound dog because, as someone knowledgeable in the rescue community told me, "All their parts are small and weird." Wouldn't you think something as good at breeding as a rabbit would possess parts that were large and easily comprehensible, like Duplo blocks?

As it turns out, I spent the better part of my free time for an entire week making calls and writing emails in order to get this information. Does this make these (at least) four nameless creatures my animals, my responsibility and/or my inglorious new hobby?

Last night, I went into the front yard to deliver dinner to the herd. The friendly rabbit was stretched out on the paving stones, its back legs kicked out behind it in a winning way, enjoying the last bit of absorbed warmth. Not three feet away was Charlotte, her body forming a striped "C" as she assiduously ignored the rabbit and pursued a nap. I freshened the water bowl and noted how the nearest bush had several pairs of black feet huddled underneath, clearly waiting for Quinn the Omniscient Predator God to leave them dinner. I served out pellets, scooped up Charlotte, put her in the garage, coaxed Lu back in the house and ejected Polly to go outside and pee.

"So, how many pets DO you have?"

All of them.

LET'S GET PHYSICAL
(PHYSICAL)

When we last checked in with Lulabelle, she was eating wet food and still bringing sexy back with the external hard drive. I think even the most churlish among us would consider this a December well spent, for a cat.

But, as many of us find out every year, winter calories don't just leave with the molting brown Christmas tree in January, picked up by the fat-sanitation department and shredded into cellulite mulch which can be packed around Nicole Ritchie in order to keep her warm. No, winter fat is more like a gopher, wrecking the stability of your lawn of self-esteem, eating the root vegetables of any hope you might have had for wearing shorts this spring.

[Note to self: In the future, read *Sunset* magazine only *after* writing blog.]

I don't know exactly what happened. Maybe Lulabelle noticed she was grooming a few more inches of stomach than she had been last summer. Maybe she saw a candid snapshot from New Year's Eve and mistook herself for an ottoman. Possibly some neighborhood cat clued her in to the fact that our new nickname for her, "La Gata Gorda", did not, in fact, translate as "Walks the Runway". Whatever triggered it, by the second week of January, Lulabelle was clearly on an exercise regimen. I respected her discipline and maturity. She didn't strap on a pair of running shoes and try for five miles the first morning, only to turn her delicate ankle and head back to the loving embrace of the hard drive. No, Lulabelle works out in a focused and aerobic way for at least forty-five minutes every day.

And by "day" I meant night.

It goes like this: Night falls. The humans read and watch a little television. Eventually, we turn out the lights and, for the most part, attempt to sleep. The cat, on the other hand— fresh as a vermin-scented daisy after an entire day of sleeping and eating things she's cornered—views the bedroom light going on as the cue to start stretching her hamstrings. Within minutes, she's doing time-trials through the house in pursuit of her prey. And what is her prey, you might ask? Is it one of the dozens of toys purchased for no other purpose than to activate feline delight?

Have you ever *met* a cat?

Lu's great pleasure is throwing, stalking, pouncing on and then killing Daughter's fuzzy ponytail holders. Having had a few weeks of late nights to contemplate this new avocation, I think I've discovered their appeal. They are little enough to be thrown and then carried around after you kill them. The fuzziness means they hang on to your claws, seemingly mocking you by refusing to die. Best of all, their very smallness means no matter how hard Quinn looks, no matter how certain she might be that she's found every rogue ponytail holder in the house, Lulabelle can always find one more for the 3:45 am "Stretch and Tone" class.

What I don't understand is how a cat who, although Super-sized, still weighs less than twelve pounds, and can make so much noise. Wouldn't you think an animal genetically wired to be a killing machine would...slink? Every night it's the Running of the Bulls at Pamplona, only with trash talking, because when Lu captures her intended prey of North American Pink-Breasted Ponytail Holder, she wants everyone to know. Since I speak only basic Cat and not all the dialects, I can only guess that her yowls and yodels translate into something along the lines of: "...who's your kitty-daddy, chump?" which segues into an exultant aria known as *All Hair-holders Bow Down Before Me*. This is usually around the time I come out from the bedroom. Lulabelle, understandably startled by the puffy-eyed homunculus lurching towards her, grabs her kill and takes off, leaping over the couch, sliding under the dining-room table, streaking through the bedrooms across the beds, and sometimes the heads, of sleeping people. This is the circuit-training part of her workout.

God help me if I try to lock the Workout Queen out of the bedrooms. Unbeknownst to me, I am her exercise buddy and Lulabelle will be *damned* if she's going through all this by herself.

INT. HALLWAY, 3 A.M. Lulabelle stands just outside the bedroom door.

LULABELLE: Qui-iii-iinnnnnn!

QUINN: Hush, Lu.

A moment of silence, while we all contemplate what an incredibly stupid thing I just said.

LULABELLE (Shouting): Quinn! Now!

QUINN: Shhhhhh!

A paw slides under the door, trying to wiggle the door open. Sensing this won't work, the paw slides back. A moment later, there is the sound of a cat's body throwing itself against the door.

LULABELLE: Hey! Quinn! Come watch me do crunches!

Over the sound of the cat hurling herself against the door, I can hear Daughter sleepily saying "...Mom-my?" and feel Consort thrashing into involuntary wakefulness. I give up, leap from the bed, and open the door. The cat, mid door-hurl, skids into the room. We stare at each other in the half-light until the cat spots something under the bed. With a crow of triumph, she darts under the box spring. The amount of noise she generates under there would indicate she has either cornered a wolverine or found another ponytail holder. I slide under the bed. In the blackness, it takes a minute to differentiate the precious target from a rubber band and a dust bunny. I wriggle back out from under the bed, walk to the door, and toss the ponytail holder into the living room. The cat races after it, screaming in joy and blood lust. I crawl back into bed and am just drifting off to sleep, so I don't hear the sound of tiny, well-exercised feet walking up to my side of the bed, right up to my head.

LULABELLE (Shouting): Throw it again! I'm firming up my butt!

On the plus side, I think the shadows under my eyes make me look mysterious. And the cat's wearing jeans she hasn't worn in years.

THE SUN HAS GONE TO BED
AND SO MUST I

Consort came to bed, waking me up. A bleary glance at the alarm clock told me it was 4:20. I was about to launch my pre-recorded "...Why do you even go to the 'Law & Order' channel?" lecture, when he cut me off.

"I was dozing on the couch," he whispered. "She kept getting up and I wanted you to get some sleep."

Even though Consort is the only male in the house, I knew exactly which "she" he meant. For the past year, Polly had been getting up every night to either pee or vomit, sometimes both. A year ago, she would get up once a night. Now, she might need to go outside three or four times between midnight and sunrise.

"How many times?"

"Five. Maybe six. I stopped counting," he said with a sigh and fell into bed.

I lay on my back and stared into the darkness. After a minute, I heard the sound of the dog's paws scrabbling on the wooden floor in the living room. She was trying to stand up. She needed to go out again. I raced to the foyer, deactivated the alarm, and raced back to the laundry room to let her out. Standing by the door, I looked up at the dark grey sky and heard the sound of our dog retching in the yard. A minute later, she stumbled in and went back to her bed. I sat at the kitchen table.

Last year, when this first become an issue, I had her checked for stomach and intestinal blockage and for diabetes. Many expensive tests later, we determined there was nothing causing the multiple trips outdoors at night. I tried only feeding her in the morning, which made her miserable and panicky, not to mention even more prone to eating trash. I tried cutting off her water after four PM, but she still needed her trips outside every night. Her back legs would randomly give out, which a vet informed me was due to a degenerative disc near her pelvis. What no one could tell me was if this was causing her pain.

She didn't act as if it caused her pain, but how could a degenerating disc *not* cause pain? I could run her through another battery of tests, with the accompanying battery of bills, but she is terrified of the vet and would probably need to be sedated for anything diagnostic, which they might not want to do for an elderly dog. And at the end of the testing, history had shown we could come back with nothing more illuminating than "...she's old, here are some pills to try. If these don't work, we can try another group of pills. But first, let's bring her back in for some blood-work..."

I couldn't remember the last time I had slept more than three hours at a stretch. Consort has a lovely job, which he enjoys tremendously, but the commute is brutal—several hours a day if the freeway Gods are angry—and he needs his rest. I couldn't ask him to do the night shift with Polly more than once a week so this was going to be my job for as long as I could stand it.

I sat in the kitchen, watched the sun rise, and thought. Every once in a while, I would gaze over at Polly on her bed. She didn't get back up. At seven, before I went in to wake up Daughter, I went into our bedroom and shook Consort awake.

"I think I'm putting her down."

Instantly awake, Consort just took my hand and rubbed it. I could hear Daughter starting to wake up. I could also hear Polly starting to try to stand, and slipping as her back legs failed.

It was now Thursday morning. I set the appointment for Friday morning. After making the call, I looked over at the dog asleep on her dog-bed and made a decision. I got her well-worn leash, jangling its hardware in a familiar summons.

"Walkies?" I said loudly.

It took a couple of calls, but my voice cut through her sleep and her hearing loss and she looked up, pleased. It took a while, but we got out to my car. We had stopped trying to put her in the SUV months ago when she misjudged the door height, fell out and cut her head. Now she was having a hard time simply climbing into my Volvo.

Consort worked from home that morning, so he joined us on our favorite hike. Years ago, when we first got her, Polly would bolt up the hill, one of us holding on to her leash and water-skiing behind her. Now, we moved at a pace best described as "stately". Her legs weren't consistent, but she seemed content.

Consort and I talked. Was it honorable to wait to euthanize her until nothing gave her pleasure and we were absolutely certain she was in constant pain? Did the fact that she could enjoy the sun on her face mean her life still had meaning? Could I hold out sleeping in patches for what might be weeks, or months? It probably wasn't years, because she was somewhere near the end of the natural life for her breed. Then again, I knew one of her ilk that lived to fifteen. Was I prepared to spend years looking for cures, trying new treatments or being her nightly chambermaid?

While we talked, the dog had slowed down considerably. Frequently during the walk, she sat down. She would try to lie down but without her padded bed to soften the fall she would get stuck. We'd haul her up again, and she'd go a few more yards. The silence grew between our rhetorical questions.

I have had pets euthanized, and it's dreadful, but it becomes infinitely worse when the decision isn't clear-cut. We could continue what we were doing, and it's pretty likely Polly would suffer before she died, if she wasn't suffering already. But if we continued on this path, Consort would suffer, as would I. I've read enough about sleep deprivation to know that I was not working at my best. Was keeping the dog alive putting Daughter in jeopardy every time I got behind the wheel? Was keeping Polly alive putting *other* people on the road in jeopardy? Even if I never hurt anyone physically, how many times had I snapped at Consort or Daughter out of nothing more than sheer grinding fatigue?

Was I keeping her alive so I didn't feel like a bad person?

Was I euthanizing her for my own convenience?

Polly was a member of our family. I treated her as kindly and lovingly as I could and kept her needs in mind at every turn. But she was also a member of a family where the other living things had needs as well. Had I been a single woman, with few obligations, I might have made another choice.

We helped her back into the car. Exhausted, she leaned against the door and fell asleep.

*　*　*

A week later, I got the call from the vet; her ashes had come back from the crematorium. Since the cat needed her vaccinations anyway, it made for a strange two-fer: yowling cat carrier in one hand, cardboard cube in the other. I noted the Cal-Pet crematorium had misspelled her name: Pollie. Somehow, this broke my heart a little more. I brought both of them home and tucked the box someplace discreet, away from Daughter's relentless purview. Monday night, I told Consort of my plans. He asked if I wanted to wait for the weekend, so he could be with me.

I thought a moment before I replied. "If it's all the same with you, I'd rather do it myself."

Consort said, "Then, let me give you something." He went to the top drawer of his bureau and brought out fragments of green paper. He held it in the palm of his hand and we both stared at it. It was half of two twenty-dollar bills, ragged and torn.

"She ate these the first year we had her. She found them on the dresser with my wallet. This is what I grabbed from between her teeth. I was furious at the time. Not so much any more. I always swore I'd bury it with her. Maybe she can use it to pay the ferryman across the river."

*　　*　　*

It was perfect hiking weather, the sun peeking flirtatiously through the leaves and trees. This time, I walked at a brisk pace. Around my wrist, I had the cord from the purple velvet bag that held the can of ashes. From a distance, I'm sure people were talking about the woman hiking in the park with the bottle of Crown Royal. I ran across a few hikers on the trail with dogs. I stopped and petted as many as I could.

We made it to the promontory that had always been our turnaround spot. I pried open the lid with my car keys and let her go. I put the slips of masticated money in the palm of my hand and blew hard. They floated off a few feet, got caught in some plants, and then tumbled down the hill.

I stood for a minute or so and then said, "Goodbye, Polly."

I turned around and went home.

I FEEL FOR YOU

As I have mentioned here previously, I volunteer with a private cat-rescue organization. I don't bring this up so my readers will think I'm a goodie-two-sneakers doling out kitty stars for public admiration. I bring this up because if you've ever been to Los Angeles and seen me someplace and thought to yourself, "Say, isn't that the former child actor whose name I can't recall! That's odd, I could swear she smells like a litter box"...

I just want to assure you that yes, I do.

On most days, I go directly home from the shelter but sometimes I stop somewhere for caffeine and if I can't find a drive-through, I will at least try to stand next to an open window. Between the stink lines rising above my clothes, the pink, runny eyes I sprout from the blizzard of dander, and the rasping noises I make trying to disgorge cat essence from my trachea, I resemble that thing small children are convinced dwells under their beds.

Week after week I have plodded in and I have cleaned. Not only do I clean cages and litter boxes, I bring sacks of laundry home with me to run through our washer/dryer. Believe me, I am not a good person. I have personally lowered the limbo pole for all sinners everywhere and yet I do believe my time in hell will be reduced by a few decades for having laundered several tons of damp, cat-infused shelter bedding during my tenure.

But this month, my nastier allergies finally trumped my nobler instincts. I couldn't spend two hours in a confined space with a few dozen cats and expect to breathe inaudibly for the rest of the day. Luckily, my histamines hit critical mass just as we had an influx of new volunteers; all clear-eyed, eager to serve, and impervious to kitty stank. I happily surrendered my on-site shift and took on another crucial responsibility: as of three weeks ago, I am the official chauffeur for cats having their Very Special Operation. You know what I'm talking about. One day you're a kitten who finds your tail endlessly fascinating. Then you start to find the tails of other cats endlessly fascinating. Suddenly you want to pick fights, put on tight clothing and go to nightclubs. That's when I swoop in and take you away for the day. After a week or so, you realize other cats aren't nearly as interesting as a really big bowl of food.

Because kitten season is in the spring we now have lots of adolescent antics going on; many teenage cats are making a spectacle of themselves. Once a week, the director of the rescue group decides which cats are their most frisky and libidinous and leaves me a message indicating who is next on the chopping block, as it were. Every Friday morning, with all the car windows open to ventilate plumes of dander and drown out the yowling, I deliver this chosen few to our offsite vet. Every Friday afternoon I pick them up and bring them home. It's the most organized thing I do every week. Or it should be.

Last Friday, I opened the shop and was greeted with a snarly mass of cats swarming around like a rebel army. It took no more than a second to determine what had happened. Usually, the volunteer who closes up at night puts food into each cage and the cats, hungry and tired after a day of glaring at one another and grooming, slink into their individual quarters and wait to be locked in. Everything is very regimented, very routine. Imagine the world's most lethargic prison, or the early-bird special at a chain restaurant in Boca. It's like that. On this previous night, however, closing shop had fallen under the command of a new volunteer, one who wasn't well versed on the ritual. So, of course, our normally well-mannered little charges turned into a horde of middle-schoolers stress-testing a substitute teacher.

Each of the cats milling around un-caged was a cat who, in the past, had shown a fondness for challenging authority figures. I could easily imagine how the volunteer spent a frustrating half-hour or so wrangling cats; cats that rewarded her with hisses and scratches before cramming themselves into the quarter-inch space behind a file cabinet. She probably thought something like, "Fine! To hell with you and your cattish ways! Go without dinner and see if I care!"

We've all been there. I didn't judge. But it did mean I was now slogging through a roiling sea of cats, hungry from not having had dinner last night and enraged that I wasn't running towards the dry food bin that very instant. I felt badly for their deprivation, but I knew another volunteer was arriving within the hour and there wasn't a cat in the place who couldn't survive that long. The cats disagreed. My ankles got nipped a couple of times but it felt less like hostile rage than pre-prandial urgency.

I grabbed the carry-cages for the cats on my chop list and looked around. I knew I was taking Bosco, Ramon and Edgar. I had no idea who Bosco and Edgar were and only the dimmest recollection that Ramon wore a natty tuxedo but this wasn't a problem as every cage has an information sheet. The first cage had a red sign indicating it was Bosco's place but when I looked inside I saw a large, elderly tabby whose man-feelings had been taken care of many years ago. A quick scan around the cages told me I had another problem beyond the cats trying to rappel up my leg to eat the breath mints in my pocket.

The volunteer from the previous night had let the cats go into whatever cages they wanted. Even discounting the cats I knew were adults and the kittens that were too young, I easily identified fifteen cats who might be Bosco or Edgar. There were three tuxedo cats, any one of which might be Ramon. Now what?

I went to each cage harboring an adolescent kitten and opened the door. The kittens, coursing with testosterone and giddy with low-blood sugar and the cry of liberty, would attempt to leap out of the cage. If the cage held only one cat, I would simultaneously stop its leap to freedom and give it a quick grope to see if I had snagged a male. For some strange reason, this always made the cat shriek in protest—a noise which folded nicely into the rest of the caged cats voicing their irritation that I was feeding *someone else* as well as the din of free-range cats who exhibited their hunger pangs by whomping one another and howling like chainsaws.

Sometimes, the first gender-feel would be inconclusive and I would have to visually examine the rear end: are those small because he's had the operation, or is he just one of those boys who are going to have to develop a sense of humor? I would make an executive decision and go either to the next cage or off in search of roommates who had propelled themselves out of the cage when I was asking him to turn his head and cough. Every few minutes, I'd peel cats off my legs and sometimes my shirt. The racket was indescribable.

After a half hour, I was beaten. I could only see out of one eye, the other being busy streaming tears so as to flush away the pound of fur a well-placed tail had deposited there. I had claw marks down my arms, my chest and my back, all of which itched and were starting to bloom. Most discouraging, I had no more information than I had before. Nearly all the adolescent cats were male, as were all three of the tuxedos. At this point, I wanted to go years before I even considered the notion of cat testicles ever again.

Through my one working eye, I saw that I had ten minutes until we were due at the vet. I felt tired and I felt vindictive. Assuming that violence and physical strength are practical indications of testosterone level, I grabbed the three half-grown cats that had clawed me the most deeply and jammed them in the cat carriers. I stacked their cages under my arms and hobbled to the door. The cats not coming with me realized I wasn't the caterer and began howling even more loudly.

Emboldened by having captured my charges—who might or might not have been Bosco, Ramon and Edgar—I turned back to the wailing throng and shouted out loud, "Really? You want a piece of me? Just ask these three tonight what happens to cats who cross me."

The new volunteers may have vigor, but we veterans have style.

MEAT PUPPETS

"Meeeeeeeeeeaaaaaaattt!!!!!"

"Meat-meat-meat-meat-meat-(inhale)-meat-meat-meat-meat-meat-meat-meat!!!!!!!!!!"

Let me bring you up to speed. A few months ago, during the tainted pet-food scare, when it looked as though Chinese manufacturers had it in for our pets, our local Whole Foods—sensing that Paranoid-Americans with discretionary income was an underserved market segment—started selling ground meat for pet food. There were several stickers on each wrapped package clearly indicating this meat wasn't fit for human consumption, which, to my thinking, is another way to say "now with more snouts and sphincters". But hey, it's better than worrying about whether the secret ingredient in your cat's *Tastee Treats* is fresh-ground melamine.

I also did the math and realized it would be no more expensive to serve Lady Hairball raw boutique meat than her favorite can of stinky wet food. But was I saving her a death from kidney failure only to put her in danger of mad-cow disease? Or ruinous whisker failure? Or some other feline-specific disorder? Not from my research. In fact, as you might suspect, the domestic cat is built from teeth to tummy, and well beyond, to consume animal protein. Their wild ancestors weren't stalking corn meal and wheat flour, two common ingredients in cat food. No, they were hunting living things. Cats are designed to look for, thrive upon, and love raw meat.

Of course, I had forgotten that cats aren't dogs. In culinary terms, dogs are the ideal guests. Whatever they find in their bowl (or on the table, or in the cats' litter box) is the *one exact thing* they had always hoped to eat. After a minute's snarfling and an enthusiastic burp, the dog trots away from the bowl, mission accomplished. The average cat is not the ideal dinner guest. The average cat is your obnoxious cousin who just got back from a six-week trip to cooking school in the south of France who glances at the sandwich you made her and sighs "You know, in *France*, they take such *care* with their food." Even with the limited range of facial expressions cats have, any change in Lulabelle's diet left her looking at me with nothing but dismay and sorrow. The first night, I hacked off a bit of pink flesh and plopped it in her bowl. She stared at me, sniffed the food and stared at me again.

LULABELLE: I can move out, you know. Just say the word.

QUINN: This is about your food, right?

LULABELLE: If you have to ask...

QUINN: What, may I ask, is wrong with it?

LULABELLE: Where's my stinky wet food?

QUINN: It was laced with fire-retardant. Look, it's meat!

LULABELLE: I hate new things. It's new.

QUINN: Not really. You eat meat all the time. It's just usually thrashing.

She sniffed it again.

LULABELLE: I have an idea what this is. Go get me stinky wet food.

QUINN: Just taste it.

LULABELLE: Or, you could open the back door. I'll just make myself an opossum.

It took a couple of days, but she started to come around. I still got the disappointed sniff for a few more days but I noticed the new food was gone within twenty minutes or so. Then, the sniff was replaced by a certain excitement when I would bring out the bag o' meat. I'd be sawing away at the frozen log of ground-up viscera that would become her dinner, and Lulabelle would be circling my legs, getting to second base with my ankles.

What I hadn't stopped to consider, because I rarely think about things from a cat's point of view, was how the excitement she had once felt about the can opener would be transferred to someone walking to the refrigerator. This makes sense because, to her way of thinking, an open fridge door and a can opener mean the same thing: imminent food.

When not opening cans of stinky wet food, we rarely used the can opener so she was correct in assuming any can-opening was a party for her. I don't want to imply we're a constantly-snacking sort of people, but I hadn't noticed how often I open the fridge until someone small and furry was there to remind me, every time:

Quinn opens fridge. Quinn feels presence. Looking down, Quinn sees Lulabelle on her hind legs, also looking in the fridge.

QUINN: Hi.

LULABELLE: Hi. Meat?

QUINN: You already had dinner

LULABELLE: So did you. And *you're* here. Meat?

QUINN: I'm shutting the fridge now.

LULABELLE: MEAT! MEAT! MEAT!

Repeat until the next feeding.

She's already developed preferences. Beef is lovely. Chicken is to be ignored until one is faint from hunger. But, if you really want to send her into ecstasies, Sister, get that cat some organ meat. I learned this the day I went to Whole Foods earlier than usual, before they'd ground their daily not-for-human selection. On a whim, I grabbed the reddest and cheapest cut of meat I could find. This turned out to be beef liver, which required cutting into smaller pieces. I was standing in the kitchen, sawing away, when Daughter walked in. She shrieked, which wasn't surprising as I was covered in blood from the elbows down and there was blood dripping on to the floor from the cutting board. Whatever she expected to find in her family's kitchen, it wasn't a scene from *Sweeney Todd.*

"Don't worry, honey," I said in what I hoped was a comforting tone as I struggled to remove a slippery blood clot from under my thumbnail, "None of this is my blood. And once I feed Lulabelle and scrub everything in this kitchen with a weak bleach cleaning-solution, this will all fade from your memory."

Having finished my butchering, I placed a quarter-cup of what looked liked Satan's erasers into Lulabelle's bowl. I opened the back door where the cat, having divined that I was preparing her dinner, flew in and made it to her bowl—about six feet away and around a corner—in one leap. She grabbed the largest hunk, threw it on the ground, pounced on it and then sang to it softly as she tore off bits. Daughter and I watched her, nervously.

Daughter whispered, "Is she supposed to do that?"

I whispered back, "I'm in very new territory here. Let's be glad that she seems happy."

Let's also be glad she hasn't figured out that every other member of her household is nothing more than a sack of organ meat, waiting to be harvested.

A CHANGE WILL DO YOU GOOD

Daughter and I were pulling into the driveway two Saturdays ago when I noticed our neighbor, Daphne, out walking her dog. I looked again and realized it wasn't her dog, a large and rather grumpy Rhodesian Ridgeback named Lucy, but a smaller, fluffier dog. I even mused out loud about why Daphne was walking someone else's dog when she spotted my car and trotted over towards our garage. At that point, any sensible person knowing my life's history would have snuck into the house, drawn the curtains and refused to answer the phone. I, however, parked the car, walked out of the garage and asked the fateful question, "So, whose dog is that?"

"I don't know," Daphne said, scratching his ears, "I found him running down the street when I was walking Lucy. He followed us home, even though Lucy kept trying to bite him. Does he look familiar to you?"

I looked at him. He was a purebred, of the sort favored by families in Dick and Jane books and little old ladies. He had a haircut, but he was dirty. He had no collar. His tail never stopped thumping. He licked my hand. "I think so," I said after a close examination of his face. "I just don't remember where he lives."

His current situation seemed blindingly clear to me. He was the coddled housedog of one of the grandmothers who had been living in our neighborhood for fifty years. These women have noisy, excitable grandchildren who visit on weekends, and who spend most of these visits slamming in and out of front doors, playing soccer in front yards and generally disrupting the domestic flow of things. I guessed that during one of those visits, our little friend here took the opportunity to go walk-about in the surrounding terrain. Someone was undoubtedly in a panic, worrying and searching for him. I looked down again. Fluff-dog and Daughter were leaning against each other in delight. Mutual hair-braiding was about to break out.

Daphne and I strategized. She worked as a bartender, which meant she'd be gone until three in the morning. In the seven hours she'd be gone, Lucy would have eaten this dog, thrown up its parts, and eaten them again. I offered to let him stay in our back yard. In the morning, we'd begin looking for the inevitable 'Lost Dog' flyers around the neighborhood. If they weren't up, which seemed inconceivable for such an affectionate purebred, we'd move to Plan B. Of course, I had no idea what Plan B would be. Daughter, upon hearing he'd be staying with us for the night, shrieked in delight and started planning his new life with us.

I said warningly, "The *night*. He's with us for the *night*. He's someone else's dog." She whispered something in his ear. He returned a knowing look. Animated hearts flew between them.

I think it's safe to say I've had more than my share of overnight canine houseguests in my back yard, and he was the best-behaved one ever, mostly for what he didn't do rather than what he did. He didn't dig a bomb crater in the lawn. He didn't produce a howl that made people in San Diego look up and say, "Did you hear that?" He didn't claw forty years of lead-based paint off the back door. He sat mutely by the back door, nose pressed in the doorjamb, waiting for anyone to emerge. If I came out to pet him or check up on him, he would flop on to my feet with a deep sigh and then try to dart into the house. "No way, little man," I would say firmly, picking him up and putting him back outside, his legs still walking mid-air, "You're not meeting the cat." The odds of him being a cat-killer were small, but it was possible. The odds of him having his nose removed by Lulabelle were all but certain.

I created a bed for him out of blankets and put out a bowl of Lucy's food that Daphne dropped off before heading for work. Eventually, he made use of both. Consort came home late that night, after having been warned of the yard-guest. When he came in, he told me the dog trotted up to him, licked his hand affably, and went back to his nest. "He seems very happy here," Consort said absently, checking the mail. "That only proves how much he's loved in his real home," I answered stubbornly.

The next morning, while waiting for Daphne to wake up, I took him and Daughter to brunch at our neighborhood cafe. His genial disposition was unaffected by multiple dog-meetings, countless friendly hands and general restaurant clatter. He was fairly adamant that my breakfast was his breakfast, but that only strengthened my suspicion he belonged to some nice old lady who gave him buttered toast every morning. I came home, expecting to see large, tear-stained "LOST DOG" signs up everywhere. There were none. Consort, on his way out, leaned over and scratched the dog's head. The dog fairly swooned. Consort glanced up at me and said, "You know, if this one stays around, that would be okay."

"Thanks, but he has a home. Someone loves him." I said firmly.

Daphne came by that afternoon. We checked out the one house we thought might have a dog of this kind and, sure enough, they did; but theirs was very much at home, grinning at us through the gate. At a loss, I made a decision for the both of us. "Take him to the shelter and have them check for an ID chip," I said to Daphne. "He won't have one, but let's just confirm that. Then we'll decide what to do next. I'd go with you, but I'd rather not, because I'm the only one home with the kid today. Taking her to a place where you can adopt animals, well..."

"Of course, of course," Daphne said quickly. "I'm just so glad you could take him last night and this morning. Just hang out. I'll call as soon as I find out."

Feeling a stab of guilt that I was making her do the heavy lifting, I heard myself say, "I'll get some writing done while you're gone. You know, on the book."

Readers, I am a horrible person. I didn't write, nor did I actually think I was going to get any writing done. I am just the kind of weasel who uses a publisher's deadline to get out of doing things.

So, did I clean? No, I did not.

Did I catch up on QuickBooks? No, I did not.

Did I clean out my athletic clothing and determine which sports bras have lost all structural integrity? Yeah...no.

Readers, I napped. It was Sunday afternoon and Daughter was attending some sort of Barbie UN in her room, and the sheets looked incredibly inviting, and I napped. I must admit this because it will weigh on me that if I hadn't suddenly been overcome with the cell-deep need to shut my eyes for just a minute, I would have taken the kid to the animal shelter with Daphne, and the next part might have gone completely differently.

I awoke a half-hour later to the phone ringing. It was Daphne, calling from her car outside the shelter, choking back tears.

"Quinn," she sniffled. "He has an ID chip. They called the owner."

Shaking my head to clear sleep from the synapses, I said in confusion, "That's good, right?"

"No," she cried. "He's mean. A real jerk. He says the dog gets out all the time. And he doesn't like him. And he's not sure if he even wants him back."

My brain scrabbled up against these facts several times without finding a toehold. The dog that had stayed with us last night didn't want to be more than four inches from my leg and adored every person he had met, including the busboy who accidentally kicked him. Daphne sounded distraught, and I was beginning to not feel too well myself, so I made excuses.

"Sure," I said confidently. "He sounds like a (male genital), but maybe he's just having a bad day. Catch me at the wrong time, and you'd think I was a total (female dog), and I'm not...Not all the time, anyway. He got the dog chipped. That has to mean something."

"He said he got the dog from a rescue group, and they did it."

I tried another tack. "Maybe he's a total (male genital), but his wife and kids love the dog." I liked that one, as it would explain the dog's affectionate stalking of Daughter and me.

"What he said was that he and his boyfriend had gotten the dog, and the boyfriend wasn't around anymore. And then he said that dogs were a lot of work."

My Achilles heel flared up. Why do some people act surprised when their pet has needs? It's not a paperback. It's a living thing. Then Daphne added, "Oh, and guess what? He claims the dog got out the day before, in Hollywood."

I sighed in disgust and uttered something unprintable. We both knew that was impossible. We're several miles from Hollywood, across major thoroughfares and a freeway. Had the dog run at full speed it might have made it to our neighborhood in a day, but a car would have run over it in the process. One of two things happened: either someone had stolen him, thinking a pure-bred was worth something and then changed their mind or, far more likely, his owner had driven to our area, removed his collar, and opened the door.

We sat in silence for a second. Daphne said apologetically, "I am so sorry to bother you with all this. I know you are trying to write."

Oh, *there's* guilt. I wondered where I put it. Had I gone with her, I would have...what? Grabbed the dog's leash from the shelter employee once we realized what a (male genital) his owner was? Offered to go to the owner's house and show him what not being liked really felt like? I would have done *something,* and while anyone who knows me can argue I might not have helped the situation, I should have been there, because something helpless needed me. And where was I?

Napping.

And lying about it.

Daphne was talking. I forced myself to focus. The owner had left things at "I *might* come get him..." The shelter gave him ten days to do so. After that, the dog was available for adoption. Daphne had stayed around until they took his picture for the website, after which an employee took the dog to a holding pen. The dog had given Daphne a look of such affection and confusion that her only option was to sit in her car for a while and cry, which is where she was when she called me.

I raced to the computer and brought up the shelter's website. There, under 'Found Dogs', was the dog, looking woeful. Points for efficiency. Under his picture was a name. I interrupted Daphne, who was fleshing out exactly what a colossal (male genital) this guy was on the phone, and said, "I'm sorry, but this is his name?"

"Yeaaaaaaaaaah", she drawled, momentarily distracted by this new evidence of the owner's general unworthiness.

"Prince Charming?"

"Yeah."

We are so changing his name, I thought, and then mentally slapped myself. We wouldn't be changing his name because he had an owner, albeit a big jerky one. And if big jerky man didn't bother to pick him up, someone else would adopt him and they would name him what they liked. I would write my book and we would continue to lead a dog-free lifestyle where paper money isn't a snack and plastic grocery bags are for groceries only.

This was Sunday. The shelter was closed on Monday, which gave me ample time to think deeply and thoroughly about the dog, in a way less visionary people would describe as obsessing. By the end of the day, I had concluded the dog was in the shelter because of me; had somehow managed to break free of the idiot who owned him but might be sent back to this idiot because of me; might not be reclaimed by idiot owner but instead be adopted by someone who would fall in love with his almost unbearable cuteness, name him Sir Lancelot, then chain him in the back yard and ignore him for days at a time, all because of me. I writhed inwardly while attending to the details of my day.

That night, Consort and I were getting ready for bed when I blurted out "I'm thinking of putting my name of the list for the dog, if you don't totally hate the idea. It probably won't matter, because the owner will probably come get it. You won't have to walk it, the kid and I will take care of the feeding—"

Consort kissed me and grinned. "I knew this one was coming back."

But that wasn't a guarantee. Overnight, I became convinced the jerk would be there at nine a.m. Tuesday to pick up the dog he didn't like. Why, you ask? Because jerks do things like that. They decide to keep something they don't want simply because it's theirs, and they paid good money for it. Or they think it's potential date-bait. Or they just need to do something really jerky today. I raced Daughter to school and arrived at the shelter at 8:54.

Needless to say, Jerk didn't arrive. I did, however, have a meeting with an adoption counselor and was deemed worthy of the dog, should it become available. In the one hour he had been viewable on Sunday, someone had already put her name on the list for him; I was second. I also had the adoption counselor add a note to the dog's file. If Jerk did arrive and was somehow capable of being talked out of taking him back, I told her, I wanted him to know the people who had kept him...what? I thought about how to phrase this best:

...Didn't have enough to do, and long to use their vacuum cleaner twice daily?

...Need one more living thing in the house with emotional needs, social peculiarities, and its own dietary restrictions?

...Have too many plastic grocery bags?

"If he does come to get the dog," I finally said, "please let him know that we loved him already."

She typed that in and then said "Okay, if he doesn't come in, we'll see you in two weeks."

Tuesday through Thursday, my day went like this:

Wake up.

Check shelter website to see if the dog was still there, or had been picked up by Jerk.

Feed Daughter.

Check shelter website to see if the dog was still there, or had been picked up by Jerk.

Take Daughter to school.

Consider buying an iPhone, so I could check shelter website while I was driving to see if the dog was still there, or had been picked up by Jerk.

Come back home.

Check shelter website to see if the dog was still there, or had been picked up by Jerk.

Write seven words for book.

Check shelter website to see if the dog was still there, or had been picked up by Jerk

And so on. My obsessive tendencies bring out the green in my eyes but otherwise serve no useful purpose. I had a stern talking-to with myself and put myself on a diet of two website checks a day. Every day, there was my little friend, looking puzzled. Daphne decided this was good news. She surmised that Jerk had moved on to winning some new paramour and not a small, familiar dog, but I refused to get my hopes up. Occasional yet persistent experience with jerks told me that it was entirely possible Jerk considered the shelter to be a relatively cheap way to board the dog and would pick him up at his convenience as the deadline approached. As the first weekend came and went, however, I allowed myself a small nightlight of hope. Jerks are all about that which is easy, and if picking up his dog on a weekend had been too much bother, it was possible he wouldn't pick it up at all. The pup still had another week in the shelter, however.

At first, I couldn't go see the dog. My guilt-bucket is very nearly full all the time, and the sight of this sweet, handsome little man, coughing and whining in his cage, cowering in terror as the tough-looking Chow/Akita mix with prison tats in the next cell terrorized him — that would have sent my guilt-bucket sloshing into the street. However, after the first weekend, I girded my loins and stopped by for a visit. I found his cage, and there he was, sitting by the gate, wiggling in pleasure at the sight of anyone walking by. He saw me right away and danced around on his hind legs. I scratched his head through the gate; he sighed in pleasure. A volunteer wandered by and said, "Isn't he the sweetest boy? I've been taking him out whenever I can." She slid her hand in, and the dog flopped on his back and slid his body against the gate, giving us both the chance to scratch his belly at once. Whatever human beings called this place, as far as Prince Charming was concerned, it was Club Med with full-body massages. At the very least, I no longer had to worry about how miserable he was in captivity. I checked with the front desk and confirmed that I was the second person in line for the dog. Someone had seen him the minute he came in on Sunday and had put her name in line to adopt him, should he become available. She was first. I was second.

Now, the only question was, what about Person #1? Oddly enough, I was okay with this dog going to another family. My job hadn't been to own him but to get him out of the street and then away from a jerk. Anyone who fell in love with him at first sight—and was vetted by the shelter—was probably as good an owner as I would be. I knew he had the potential to be a great dog but I had no space in my life that needed filling. I had a child. I had after-school activities. I already had a pet. I had an old house developing conditions like osteoporosis of the joists. I had a hobby (writing a blog). I had a job (writing a book). Sure, I had a dog-bowl, a leash and a chew-toy, but that didn't make me someone looking for a dog; that made me someone with a sentimental streak. I liked this dog but I certainly didn't need this dog.

Still, I still checked the website twice a day. I didn't really think about Jerk anymore. I just liked looking at his little face. Daughter knew we might be getting a dog, and we might not be getting a dog. He was ours, unless he wasn't. Consort took to referring to him as Schrodinger's Dog. I asked Daughter if she had any thoughts for a name. She answered swiftly and confidently: Rupert. Where she got this I'll never know, but it suits him and it's miles less girly than Prince Charming. If the dog ever got out and Consort needed to shout after it around the neighborhood, his masculinity would remain intact. As luck would have it, the day the dog became available was one of those days where Daughter's school was closed for no apparent reason—something like *Teacher Enrichment Conference* or *Teacher Preparedness Enrichment* or *Conference for Preparing Enrichment*, which could also be pronounced *We're Tired of Your Children*. So, either way, she was available to come with me.

Our time-slot for claiming him was 9:30 to 10:00. We arrived at 8:59 because I am pathologically punctual and because if the first person on the adoption list did, in fact, show up on time, we wanted to be able to say goodbye to him. I figured the least I could offer Daughter was closure and a pie-and-milkshake breakfast afterwards, to ease any sadness. We sat on the bench in the front room and watched a few dogs come in, a couple of dogs get adopted. At 9:25, our adoption counselor came out and smiled at us. "I'm guessing she's not coming," she said. "Should we go get your dog?"

Daughter gasped in glee, and I thought Holy Crud, I'm getting a dog! During all of this, I hadn't exactly thought things through to this point. I had visualized Jerk coming back, or Person #1 arriving at exactly nine and swooping the dog up in her arms. It just hadn't occurred to me we'd get to someone handing me the dog. I knew from the information sheet on his cage that his adoption-list was full. After me, there was a 10:00, and then a 10:30, all the way through 4:00. A bunch of people wanted this dog.

For a second, I thought about grabbing Daughter's small arm and dashing for the door, keeping my relative freedom while knowing someone would take the dog. But, I thought, what if everyone else bails, and he's still here tomorrow? What if the person takes him, changes their mind, and decides to leave him back in my neighborhood again? What if my family, flawed and hectic as it is, is the best home he would ever know?

"Yes," I heard myself saying, looking down into Daughter's shining eyes. "Let's go get our dog."

I WANT TO BE LAZY LIKE THE
DOGS IN THE YARD

So, the dog.

I can say with certainty that his former owner was not only a (male genital), he was also an idiot. Rupert lives to be easy. He is house-trained and he is crate-trained, if a bit grumbly about it. He let me wash and groom his paws, which is good because one of us is a little furry and likes walking through unspeakable things. He lets people take his food away from him. On our second day with Rupert, a toddler offered him a cookie and I let out a small horrified squeak because not only would our last dog, Polly, have snatched the cookie, she would have swallowed the kid's arm up to the elbow, just to make sure she wasn't leaving behind any crumbs. Polly ate any food, any time. Frankly, she ate a lot of things that weren't exactly food. They weren't even food if you were stuck on a lifeboat for a very long time and had already eaten your Reeboks and reclaimed seagull feathers. Polly ate FedEx envelopes, plastic bags, two twenty-dollar bills, packs of needlepoint needles and a baby sock. I know she ate the sock because, while I didn't see her eat it, I saw her pass it. It wouldn't leave easily, and the sensation of it hanging halfway out frightened her so much that she ran in from the back yard and dashed around the house in a panic, the unspeakable second tail flapping behind her like a pennant.

So now, having been trained by a Dalmatian, I lunged towards the cookie-wielding child and tried to remember the basic rules of applying a tourniquet. Rupert, however, considered the cookie for a moment took it gently from the child's hand and ate it with a delicacy you'd associate with your better class of debutante. He adores children. The finest visual he has given me so far was when we took him to a park with a group of Daughter's friends and he spent a crisp autumn afternoon chasing and being chased by six shrieking eight-year olds. His grin wrapped halfway around his head.

This is not to say that he's perfect. He is a bit stubborn, which I understand and accept. I'm stubborn. Consort is stubborn. Daughter is stubborn. We're a household full of individuals who know things would go so much better if you would only do what I say. I've had dogs that were aggressively stubborn and I've had dogs that were sneakily stubborn. I know how to deal with those. Rupert, however, is cheerfully stubborn. Here's an analogy: Years ago, a friend-of-a-friend took a sales job at a home electronics store. His job-training manual advised him to "...consider the word 'No' as a request for more information." Besides giving you some sense of why men in clip-on ties follow you through the media department, yammering about the virtues of a particular plasma TV, this also give you some insight as to what it's like to discipline our new dog:

Monday, 10 a.m. Rupert is on the couch. Quinn enters the room and sees Rupert on the couch.

QUINN: Off!

RUPERT: What?

Quinn grabs the dog by the collar, pulls him off couch, while saying "OFF!" firmly.

RUPERT: Um, what was that all about?

QUINN: We don't have dogs on couches around here. Here's your bed. It's made of 73% recycled material. It's soft and comfy. It was shockingly expensive. Use it.

RUPERT: Oh, this is lovely. Thank you. And thanks for the heads-up on the "No-couch" thing.

QUINN: Hey, no problem.

Monday. 10:15 a.m. Quinn comes out from the office to find the dog on the couch.

QUINN: OFF!

RUPERT: Pardon me?

QUINN: OFF!!

Quinn grabs Rupert by the collar, pulls him off.

RUPERT: Still?

QUINN: Not still. Always.

RUPERT: Really? Because I could have sworn you said I could be on the couch right about...now.

QUINN: No.

RUPERT: Okay, I guess there was a misunderstanding. I'll just sit here on the dog-bed until you go back to work.

QUINN: All...right.

Quinn walks into office, and then quietly pokes her head out. As soon as Quinn leaves the room, the dog darts back towards the couch. As he puts his front paws on it...

QUINN: OFF!

RUPERT: This is news to me.

Days of this, I tell you. He's some kind of canine-martial artist, using my own desire for furless furniture against me. But he has me mistaken for someone who hasn't been trained by the sensei of evasive badgering: my daughter. I made it through a year of "...*but all the other girls got the Bratz bordello, why can't I?*"without caving in. I'll keep this dog off the couch.

The cat, however, was having a rough time adjusting. I considered writing about the new-dog experience from the cat's point of view but decided not to, as it would be impossible to pull off while keeping my promise of working clean.

For the first week, since I had no knowledge of his history with cats, I had to assume Rupert might harbor hidden, cat-murderous impulses so I made absolutely certain the old cat and the new dog were never alone together. Further complicating matters, this adjustment period took place in weeks leading up to Halloween, the one time of year when Lulabelle, a black cat, isn't allowed to go outside for her own good. So the new dog and the tenured cat were trapped inside the house together but never allowed to see one another. This was "Big Brother" as constructed by the Witness Protection Service.

All of Lulabelle's days were spent in Daughter's room, unless we were home, when we could shut the hallway door from the rest of the house and she could at least have the run of the bedrooms and bathrooms. The dog could have the rest of the house. Of course, this meant both of them spent nearly all their time at the door separating them, like Pyramus and Thisbe, sniffing deeply. The cat's hair didn't un-puff for a week. Slowly, with tons of security, a tight leash and multiple escape possibilities for the cat, I allowed them to see one another.

By week two, the cat and I were starting to suspect Rupert didn't mean her any harm. If anything, his enthusiasm for her resembled less predator meets prey, and more pre-pubescent girl meets Hannah Montana. The very sight of Lulabelle's tail, swishing around the corner into Daughter's room, would send the dog into barking raptures and whirling in circles. The few times he actually made eye contact with her, he threw himself into the play-position: butt up in the air, tail spinning dervishly. Had Lu been on tour, Rupert would have paid anything to see the show and buy the t-shirt.

The cat, having gotten over her initial apprehension, settled into a deep and predictable level of contempt. If this dog wasn't going to kill her, she seemed to think, then it needed training. She's very good at dog training but I doubt Cesar Milan or the Monks of New Skete should worry about competition just yet. Lulabelle's entire training philosophy is based on the simple premise that a very sharp claw, precisely hooked into a dog's nose, gets the dog's attention. This is her answer to nearly everything the dog does.

Run at the cat and invite her to play? Get a nail in the nose.

Decide to sit up on your hind legs and watch the cat eat her dinner on the clothes dryer? Nail in the nose.

Having observed the cat jump up on the couch, realize you can get really comfortable and cuddle with your new best friend? Nail in the nose. Also, someone shouts "Off!" at you.

The whole week of training can be summed up by the sound of dog-nails clicking against the wooden floor, then the sound of a hiss, then the sound of a dog yipping, then the sound of dog-nails clicking off in the other direction. I added my part by shouting, "Leave it!" whenever he would start to drift towards her, which might have helped the training or it might have merely increased the resting noise-level inside the house. Either way, I suspect the carefully inserted nail-of-negative-reinforcement did more than any human command ever could.

We're now three weeks into the process. Last night, I caught them both hanging out in the hallway outside the bathroom, watching Daughter brush her teeth. They were actively ignoring one another, which feels not unlike progress. Still, about once a day, the dog looks over and thinks "Cat! I shall touch her with my nose!" I then hear:

Click-click-click-click-click-click-click-click-HISS-YIPE!-Click-click-click-click-click-click-click...

Around here, that's the sound of a functional family.

CAN'T ANYBODY FIND ME
SOMEBODY TO LOVE

The new dog, Rupert, is doing very well, thanks for asking.

I keep waiting for the crazy to slither out and, say, eat the armoire but there doesn't appear to be any crazy in him. There are only doe-eyes, a constantly wagging tail and the most uniformly happy disposition ever seen outside a cult. His demands are simple: he wants to be with us. More specifically, he wants to be with me. After living with an erratically moody Dalmatian dowager for six years, it's odd to be adored.

Polly, the spotted diva, actually preferred my mother's company to mine. Whenever I took her to visit my mom, I'd have to drag her from the house, front legs wrapped around my mother's waist, moans of anguish letting the world know I was ripping her away from the only mother she had ever known. Rupert loves my mother, as he loves everyone who tells him he's a sweet boy and in the proper light resembles Orlando Bloom. But I'm the only poster inside his locker.

When you get a new dog and you have the kind of friends I have, you go through something like a weeks-long baby shower. I'd bring Rupert to meet people. People would come to meet him. People would coo over him. And people would bring him presents. Unlike when Daughter was born, no one has yet to give me burp towels, which is good, because I never did understand what I was supposed to do with them.

What my friends did bring were dog-toys and chewies, and these are both completely appropriate and always welcome. He has taken all of them to his bed and frequently tries to bring them up onto the couch. But his great love right now is a toy I found in the "slightly-dented-and-drooled-upon" discount bin at the local pet store. It is a fuzzy, stuffed lizard in a shade of blue that offends even the blind. Embedded its plump middle is a squeaker. He loves his lizard toy almost as much as he loves me. In truth, he might love Lizard more because I eventually complain if he drools on me or jumps on the couch but Lizard never does. At least once a day, he races off to find Lizard, delivers it to me, and we have a rousing game of fetch until one of us has to go back to writing or needs a cup of tea.

Lulabelle the cat observes all of this with unambiguous contempt. She is long past worrying whether or not the dog is going to hurt her. A few needle-sharp swipes to the nose has taught him to give her a wide berth. Nevertheless, she watches him go about his canine undertakings with a visible disdain—a certain curl to her upper lip. I'm pleased about this because, while I have no hard science to back this up, a lifetime's observation of cats leads me to believe that every cat needs something to hate. It focuses them. Otherwise, the day-to-day existence of the average housecat is nothing more than a tedious stream of needs met and butts scratched. Having an object in their lives that fills them with disgust provides something to write about in their journal. And as far as Lu is concerned, this dog might be the perfect manifestation of inanity.

At least once a day, the dog makes social overtures:

INT. LIVING ROOM. DAY. Rupert ambles up to Lulabelle, who is grooming her bikini area.

RUPERT: Hi!

Startled, the cat snaps her head around and glares at the dog.

CAT: W....h....a...t...?

RUPERT: You look especially pretty today. Did you do something new with your ears?

CAT: (Raising one paw) Do you need the nail?

RUPERT: You're busy. I'll check in later.

Yesterday, the dog produced Lizard and shook it in front of me in a tantalizing manner. I knew the cue and said sternly, "Drop it."

We're back in obedience training and the new teacher advocates hand-signals rather than words. She swears that when we think dogs are listening to what we say, they're actually picking up on body language, so we might as well go directly to the hand-signal. This is fine, but we haven't gotten to the signal for "Leave it," so I went with the tried-and-true stern voice and waiting.

After a minute or so, the dog dropped the lizard and I picked it up while singing "GOOD dog!" I then flung Lizard across the room.

If joy has ever had a physical form, it was Rupert, nails scrabbling to find traction on the hardwood floor, racing after his favorite toy. He pounced on Lizard and brought it back to me, tail waving proudly. For centuries, his ancestors retrieved buckshot birds back from the marsh to their owners' feet, but no dog was ever more proud than my dog was of his plush, electric-blue quarry. So pleased was he, in fact, that while he ran away from me towards Lizard, and ran back to me with Lizard, he flew past the cat no fewer than eight times. The first few passes, the cat went to the trouble of arching and puffing up her fur at the galloping beast headed in her direction who clearly meant her harm. By lap six, she wasn't arching or puffing any more. She was icily watching him bound back and forth, flipping her tail in the measured way cats do when they're focused on something peculiar. If anything, she seemed a little miffed at being ignored.

Each time Rupert raced past the cat, she shifted a little closer to his line of travel. Each time, focused on his prize, he paid no attention to her. Finally, throwing her dignity to the wind, she stepped nearly in front of his path. Flush with the pleasure of having caught Lizard yet again, he dropped it in front of her, threw his butt in the air and barked happily. Lulabelle swatted him sharply on the nose and walked away, tail and head held high. Undaunted, he picked up the toy and brought it to me and dropped it at my feet.

I picked up Lizard, scratched the dog's head and said to him, "If it's any consolation, I think she likes you."

I'm inclined to agree with the trainer that dogs don't understand spoken English.

Still, he seemed pleased.

FREE YOURSELF

We here at Casa Quinn are very much being ourselves these days. This is more attractive on some of us than others. Daughter, for example, is being purely herself and being herself fits her like a wee little couture Chanel suit that is also stain-proof and comes with its own matching soccer ball. I will go out on a limb and say no one in this house is better at being a young girl than she is. Were she not so busy being a young girl she could run weekend seminars in how to be the best young girl you could be; she's just *that* good.

Consort is also being himself, with a few exciting developments. Because I am in the last uphill climb writing the first draft of the book, he has nobly offered to take Daughter to school every morning so that I can write during the time of day when I am least stupid. This is a noble offering because, as I have mentioned before, similar to hamsters and the Aye-Aye of Madagascar, Consort is a nocturnal creature. I arrange everything the night before— including Daughter's clothing and the coffee maker—so in the morning he has to do nothing more than a controlled fall through the house and into the car. How he drives while still deep in a REM cycle is a conversation he can someday have with an employee of the California Highway Patrol. In sum, Consort is perfectly himself, only before 9 a.m., which makes him even more attractive than he was to begin with.

Lulabelle the cat is very good at being herself and I have the body bags to prove it. When I read about how certain birds and soft-bodied mammals on the islands of Hawaii were completely exterminated by the introduction of the domestic cat, I think of Lulabelle. If I could keep her inside forever, I would. But that would involve none of the rest of the family ever opening a door or a window, even for a second. Eventually, we must take out the garbage or sign for a package, and Lady Death slips out the door, as relentless as an agent of Shin Bet. In truth, were we to never open the door, she would amuse herself by killing and eating us and then growing her own thumbs so she could open the door and go out and kill other things. At least once a week, she leaves us something dead by the back door. Sometimes, the dead whole thing is inches from a dead half thing and some feathers from a totally different thing. If there are any birders reading this, I am so sorry. We belled her, but it doesn't seem to slow her down one bit. All it means is that several times a week, some little bird's last thought is: "Say, what's that ring—"

Lulabelle gets rats and mice, too. Piles of them. But I don't think anyone is too upset about those. The yard was bad enough, but she's stepped up her game. Lately, she's started bringing her take-out home. The first one was under the bench in the bedroom, which answered that long-simmering question: "What is the thing I *least* want to see next to my balled-up sock first thing in the morning?"

The next violation came to my attention because Daughter, doing something perfectly innocent and girlish in her room, suddenly called out for me. Her words were unintelligible but I caught from her tone it wasn't: "I'm having a wonderful time and just wanted you to know it."

"What is it?" I hollered from the kitchen, where I was cleaning out the spice cabinet.

[I will do anything to avoid writing.]

"I said," she explained patiently, sticking her head into the kitchen. "Lulabelle has a dead bird in my bedroom, behind my hamper."

I stared down at the pre-lapsarian jar of Juniper berries in my hand and sighed.

"Is it dead or just hurt?" I asked, stalling. Hard to decide which prospect was less appealing.

"It's dead, I hope," she said. "Because Lu's eating it."

My softhearted, animal-centric daughter had somehow developed a Marlon Perkins' indifference towards her bloodthirsty cat. This was zoological realpolitik. Lu ate things, many of which were cute before they were eaten, and Daughter would blithely hum *The Circle of Life* then move on with her day. Leaving feathers and wet bits behind the hamper was abusing the privilege, though.

I did what any right-thinking person would do. I found Consort and handed him a plastic bag. The way I see it, I was in labor with Daughter for forty hours and, therefore, never have to scrape up small, dead things. I did, however, sweep up feathers after the coroner left. The cat, which had been removed from the room and the feast, was allowed back in after cleanup. The dog and I followed her in, me to check for any leftover beaks and toes, him because the combination of my proximity and the cat's proximity guaranteed a perfect time. Lulabelle ran to where she had left her bird and, finding it missing, turned around and slapped the dog. When anyone in this house is being true to their nature, they are assigning blame.

Rupert has been true to his nature and we're all puzzled. Each pet, as with each child, arrives with their own needs, passions, and peculiarities. Unlike a child, a pet cannot tell you why certain things matter, or must be shunned at all cost. You, as the owner, can only say "*that*, Dog, is a thing you do". Or you can find the thing they do so crazy-making that you spend months screaming at them, reading books, watching hours of pet-training shows on cable TV, hours more pet-training videos on YouTube, and then trying every behavior-modification technique you can unearth. After all that effort — all that wasted effort — you finally say to them "*that*, Dog, is a thing you do".

Rupert is a far more refined chap than your average dog. Not for him the dark delights of the cat's litter box, or the counter-surfing for an entire pork shoulder. But as with many of your more refined individuals, there are some eccentricities. His great calling in life is to bring me Daughter's stuffed animals. He wakes up in the morning, has a quick bite and dashes off to work. Before my tea has even steeped, he has trotted into her room, gotten up on his hind legs and gently removed a stuffed animal from her sleeping arms. Graceful as a pickpocket, he leaves Daughter still asleep and the rest of her menagerie unmolested. Finding me in the kitchen, he drops it at my feet and, unless restrained, goes back in for another one. I'll grab the first three and be taking them back in when he'll pass me in the hallway, bringing out a fourth.

Polly would take the occasional fluffy love-object of Daughter's, but that was only in preparation of eviscerating it entirely and following it up with an amuse-bouche of spork. Rupert carries the stuffed animals with the tender attention of a mother lion, doing them no greater harm than a tolerable deposit of moisture and a wisp of dog-breath. We have procured his own plush toys and he likes them very much, thank you, but his need to move Daughter's stuffed animals cannot be reasoned with or displaced onto other targets. His breed was shaped for generations to retrieve and somewhere, in the depths of his brain, this need is calling the shots. He loves me and has determined the only way I can truly be myself is with a fun-fur ziggurat constructed in my honor around my ankles.

PIRATE SHIPS WOULD LOWER THEIR FLAGS WHEN PUFF ROARED OUT HIS NAME

Today's QC Report is brought to you by:

DRAGONS! RIGHT OUTSIDE! HUGE DEMONS WALKING AROUND! SHOOTING POISONOUS FLAMES FROM ORIFICES BOTH TRADITIONAL AND UNEXPECTED!

At least, that's what the dog tells me.

He's such a nice dog, our Rupert. He's genial to a fault, attractive without overplaying it and produces slightly less than the usual amount of gas for his kind. He has only two foibles: One, he's still pretty certain that I not only will allow him on the couch but actually secretly long for him to be on the couch, such that my lips might say "No, no" but there's "Yes, yes" in my eyes.

Since my lips are, in fact, saying "OFF!" and saying it loudly and regularly, I am puzzled as to what mixed signals I am giving off. Perhaps he takes my running around the house looking for car keys as a coded signal that everything I've just said means nothing.

When I first mentioned this habit in an earlier post, a woman wrote in to explain his habit of jumping on the couch when I'd left the room for longer than thirty-five seconds was an indication of his respect for my being the alpha bitch in the household. I have no reason not to believe this, but if I get him a t-shirt that says *My mommy thinks I'm very important in my own special way* can I please have a couch which doesn't have a permanent, dog-sized divot cushioned in a nest of fur?

No?

All right, then.

His less frequent, yet far more aggravating misbehavior is Dragon Patrol. I have had dogs nearly my entire life and every one of them hated something outside our house with a rage so searing it would cause them to grow more teeth so they could snarl meaner. One dog hated the sound of VW Beetles, viciously barking at the street long after the offending vehicle had entered another area code. Another dog hated one specific dog that had the temerity to get walked past our house every day. All other dogs could pass, but not this one. The two dogs could meet on the sidewalk and be as agreeable as two chums from the Ladies' Auxiliary, but if my dog was inside and this dog was outside, *someone needed to die.*

Polly despised skateboarding teenagers hanging out on the sidewalk using our driveway for half-pipe practice. She viewed them working out new ways to injure themselves as a blight shaped by Satan to annihilate all that is good. Coincidentally, this is also Consort's reaction to skateboarding teenagers. When the boarders would start clustering, I would crate the dog and go out to shoo them away. If they didn't shoo, I would send Consort and the dog out to be so generally irritable that even hormone-saturated adolescent boys with untreated concussions would choose another venue.

But in each case, I *knew* what made the dog nuts. I'd live with it. I'd work around it. Periodically, I would dole out Rescue Remedy, a homeopathic pet tranquilizer. Rupert, however, is an enigma, wrapped in a puzzle, sporting a handsome collar. Once a day, he flies to the nearest window and gets very, very upset. His fur bristles. He bares his teeth and barks. Oh, does he bark. He barks for about ten minutes. And while I love him very much, I cannot say that he has the most masculine bark in the world. I'm thrilled that he's neutered, but did they have to do such a thorough job? It's a ten-minute operetta to home security directed by Tiny Tim.

But here's the thing: there's *nothing* outside. I mean it. Not a single stinking thing that should be setting him off. Not a moving car. Not a person. Not a dog. Not even a sheet of drywall leaning impudently against a trash container. I know enough of the canine mind to look for the taunting squirrel or the neighborhood cat making rude gestures from behind a nearby branch, but neither exists. Rupert can be in the back yard, or the front door, or any window in the house. The barking can happen first thing in the morning or after midnight. The only thing all these barking fits have in common is that there is nothing out there.

At first, I thought it was just that I didn't move fast enough and had missed whatever demon it was out there that was driving him to fits, but then I noticed he would see me and try to bring me in on it. We'd then have several fabulously unproductive minutes of my saying "What is it?" and his saying "BARK!" until it would occur to me to get more information. In the beginning, I would descend into reasoning with a dog, because that *always* goes well. Sooner or later, one of us would end up in the crate for a few minutes, waiting for our homeopathic canine tranquilizer to kick in.

Every day, for a few minutes, at a point that is as abundantly clear to him as it is maddeningly erratic to me, Rupert has to lose his mind. Having consulted with dog-training manuals, I learned that I was supposed to ignore him during these episodes. This was easier to manage when his mind-losing was in the back yard than it was when he was between me and the television. One night a few weeks ago, the day's crazy bark came upon him when he was standing next to my bed. Because I was sleeping at the time, I didn't take this particular eruption with a saintly degree of loving tolerance. I decided that ignoring him was not an option at this exact moment and was about to drag him off to the crate when I caught a look at his eyes. Under his sumptuous lashes, he was terrified. My heart softened. He came to our house four months ago already fully-grown. He's experienced things, and I'm guessing not all of them were pleasant. I scratched his head.

"Dragons again, dude?" I said. He thumped his tail. "Thanks for the warning,"

He still has one Dragon fit a day. Out of habit, I still look outside, expecting to see something. Whatever he sees is warned off by his fierce falsetto and after a few minutes he lies down near my feet, having saved his new family and new home yet again.

JINGLE ALL THE WAY

I take Benadryl for my allergies.

Consort takes Benadryl for his allergies.

The dog takes Benadryl for his allergies.

When it comes to Benadryl, we buy in bulk.

When I took Rupert in for an exam, not long after he first arrived, the vet pointed out his runny eyes and the red skin between his toes. "Allergies," he declared and I was not surprised. The dog's nightly scratching, accompanied by the gypsy music of his jingling tags, had become our evening lullaby. The vet offered several suggestions, the cheapest and easiest of which was Benadryl. Two pills. Every day. Because I am fond of the cheap and the easy, I took Rupert home and promptly popped a pink and white pill into his mouth. I massaged his gullet firmly, felt him swallow, and we all went on our way. I felt smug in that *look at me getting things accomplished* way. He appeared stunned, but cheered himself up with a long, noisy scratch.

An hour later, I found a slightly chewed pink and white pill on the ground. I picked it up, first puzzled and then challenged. Hide your pill in your cheek will you? "We'll just see about that", I said out loud, summoning my inner Nurse Ratched.

Minutes later, I'd tucked another capsule in some peanut butter and summoned the dog using my most cheerful "It's possible I have some steak for you" tone. The offering was gratefully accepted; the chewy anti-histamine surprise in the middle went down without comment. I didn't find it later, and the scratching seemed less vigorous. Success!

Twice a day, I would assemble this peanut-butter delivery system and twice a day, he would uncomplainingly take his meds. The fun of watching a dog eat peanut butter was just an added bonus. What wasn't an added bonus was observing any positive effect on his symptoms. After the first day or so, not only did his prescription not seem to be working, he seemed to be scratching more, and chewing at his paws with renewed vigor. All through the day and into the night, I would hear his tags jingling — a percussive reminder that the problem wasn't being fixed at all. I mentioned this problem to a friend who knew dogs. She asked a few questions, and when I got to the "He certainly likes his peanut butter" part, her hand flew to her mouth in dismay.

So. It seems many dogs are allergic to peanuts. Giving him an antihistamine in an outer shell of super-histamine might not be moving the ball forward. They can also be allergic to wheat, soy and corn, otherwise known as the

Three Horsemen of Kibble. I could take him in for expensive tests or, as my friend suggested, cut everything with peanuts, wheat, soy and corn from his diet, continue the Benadryl, and see if the itching stopped. Since I already had him on a raw-meat diet, this wasn't a huge transition but I did have to check the labels of all of the nibbly-treats I had been using for obedience training. A half-hour later, I'd determined that only one of his treats was completely free of peanuts or any of the offending fillers. I also determined I wouldn't be getting that half-hour back at the end of my life. I bought him allergen-free treats, which were gaspingly expensive. Benadryl might have been an easy fix, but it certainly wasn't cheap anymore.

And we were still back to the original problem. Rupert has a world-class talent for not taking pills. At first, I tried insinuating the pill in a little chunk of meat, only to discover the dog could remove all the delicious meaty bits with his tongue, leaving a virtually unmarked pill in his bowl, mocking my very existence. I then tried putting the pill down his throat and holding his jaw shut with one hand while massaging this throat with the other and also petting his back. Yes, you see the problem here; I was so desperate for an itch-free life that I evolved a third hand. Fat lot of good it did me. Or the dog. Later each day, I'd find a moist and dented capsule being batted around the living room floor by the cat.

One morning, Rupert came in to wake me up. He put his paws on the bed and, next to my focusing eyes, gently dropped a Benadryl next to my pillow. He then sat down on the ground and scratched. Jing-jing-jing... I leapt from the bed, snatched up the pill, and grabbed him in a headlock. Wedging his mouth open, I crammed in the pill as deep as my fingers would allow and commenced to throat-rubbing. Consort squinted awake at this point and, blinking, took in this latest domestic tableau.

"I'll be doing this for a while," I explained. "You'll need to make the kid's breakfast."

One of the unexpected benefits of morning communication with a night-person is that they are very accepting. All behavior displayed before 10 a.m. — be it Reiki for dogs or simply eating breakfast — strikes them as equally incomprehensible. Consort stumbled out of bed and weaved towards the kitchen. Rupert and I stared at one another. His eyes were gazing up at me reproachfully but at least they seemed less runny.

"Just take the pill, dude," I said softly to him, fondling his esophagus. After a few minutes, I declared him adequately pilled and let him up. He trotted off quickly before I could change my mind. Rupert is a dog with simple needs. He needs to be loved, to eat expensive food, to scratch deeply and fully, and to find a private place in which to jettison another pink and white invader.

TRAPPED IN THE CLOSET

First, to everyone who sent *get-the-pill-down-the-dog's-throat-and-keep-it-there* suggestions, I cannot thank you enough. This confirms my suspicion that my readers are all kind, knowledgeable and persistent. It also gives me pleasure to imagine people throughout the world asking themselves, "Now, where did I put the dog's pill-shooter?"

I will mention that liquid Benadryl makes a marvelous canine beard-styling gel and pill-hiding milk products like cheddar and cream cheese make certain dogs volcanically flatulent. A week ago, I didn't know these things and now I do. I've amended my antihistamine protocols accordingly.

Contrary to every single parent-teacher conference my mother ever attended, it seems I *am* capable of learning something. Through trial-and-error-and-error-and-trial-and-a-few-more-errors, I have discovered a surefire method for getting the dog to take a pill. This involves shoving my hand so far into his digestive system that I can probably check his prostate. Then I remove my hand and enjoy a nice long, obsessive hand washing.

Usually, on the way to scrub my hands I pass by the hallway closet. If there is such a thing as a warm and welcoming hallway closet, this isn't it. It's narrow and tall and, weirdly enough, seems deeper than the length of its adjacent hallway. We merely assume there is a back wall somewhere in its shadowy recesses but we cannot say for sure. I have wondered on more than one occasion if this closet isn't a portal to some not-terribly-friendly parallel universe. Either way, we relegate to its shadowy maw the large, the ungainly, the out-of-season, and the vacuum cleaner; our assumption being that should malevolent, extra-dimensional creatures somehow tumble into our world, they will be foiled by a bulk package of toilet paper falling on their conjoined heads, a winter coat wrapping around their barbed tentacles, or a vacuum cleaner being a vacuum cleaner and somehow obstructing their progress. It's a dim and dusty space crammed with bags and boxes, many of which are completely unknown to me, which leads me to suspect these objects have reached sexual maturity and are now breeding. The closet is also crammed to capacity. There is room inside for nothing larger than a single ski mitten or an empty manila envelope. And yet, every week, Lulabelle the cat insists on slipping through the door whenever one of us goes in search of TP or a light bulb. She will then get trapped inside when the door closes behind her and spend a few hours in its murky depths, unbeknownst to any of us.

I'm not sure whether this reflects worse on her or me. She's not small. Shouldn't I be capable of noticing a football-shaped cat leaping past my ankles as I drag out the vacuum cleaner or a box of random crap? Since she does this at least once a week, wouldn't you think I'd remember to make a brief survey of the closet before shutting the door? But, readers, I do. I *do* keep an eye out for her. I *do* check to make sure she isn't scaling her way up a cashmere coat or having a contemplative chew on the holiday ribbons. Before I shut the door, I scan the closet to ascertain whether or not she's in there. Believe me, I look. Hours later, when I've returned to the back door for the eighth time to let in the cat, I can hear plaintive mewing from somewhere not outside, but inside. Then it hits me like a bag of snow boots: the closet! I open the door and she comes stomping out, brushing the metaphorical dust off her theoretical shoulders. And while a cat looking indignant is always entertaining, I can't say I feel much guilt over her involuntary confinement.

In fact, I'm starting to think she might not be as smart as she appears. Bright shiny eyes and the ability to kill anything less than two feet tall notwithstanding, she is starting to remind me of my friend who kept dating drummers. After the fifth or sixth time Lulabelle got locked into someplace dark for an entire afternoon, wouldn't you think she'd develop some neural shortcut which, upon seeing the closet door open before her, would light up: *Move on, nothing to see here.* And let's not forget that Consort and Daughter leave other closet doors open all the time. Since this makes me nuts on a par with chewing on tinfoil, I spend a lot of time closing closet doors. Out of habit, I always check inside. Am I locking the cat in this one or that one? Never.

To Lulabelle, all other closets are jejune, obvious destinations, not worthy of her attention. A typical inventory of clothing, shoes and the more predictable closet fare holds no appeal whatsoever. Only the magical midnight hallway closet with its three cubic inches of available space and its glorious musty smell must be thoroughly reexamined.

But then: Shock! The door closes and she is locked inside the closet! Who could have possibly foreseen this? Having no night-vision camera in there I'm just guessing, but I imagine she reads the label on the 55-gallon drum of Murphy's Oil soap we got at Costco, whiffs a few mothballs and passes out for a couple of hours. Upon awakening, she notices that she's hungry and commences to mewl pitifully until I let her out.

The last time I sprung her free, on an impulse I picked her up and switched on the closet light. Together, we stared into the depths. When I put her down, she dashed off towards her food dish but then turned and looked back into the closet. Something galvanized her attention and she slinked back towards its siren's call.

I grabbed her round little body and tucked it under my arm. "No more closet today, you nitwit," I said to her. But I wasn't mad. She has a brain no larger than a walnut, I thought to myself, scratching between her ears. And not the whole walnut, just the inside meat part. I considered this as I transported her away from closet-temptation and back to her food dish. She's a simple creature, lacking a human's ability to reason, to strategize, to adjust to new information. She will continue to do the same thing again and again because it is in her limited nature.

In the kitchen, something caught my eye: a half chewed Benadryl sitting in the middle of the floor. I didn't need to see the cat's smirk. I could feel it.

COME RAIN OR COME SHINE

Yesterday morning the sun was shining fully with only a few wisps of grayish cloud business over the distant mountains. The newspaper and weather.com both swore we were in for it, rain-wise, by noon. But I'd been punked before. Too many times I had sent Daughter to school wearing enough rain gear to protect the Lincoln Memorial because the weather pundits promised a monsoon downpour, only to pick her up that afternoon, squinting against the unfiltered sunlight and trudging to the car in rain boots and floppy hat. Clouds will do what they will, and even the most seasoned meteorologist can get it wrong. In order to dress Daughter correctly, I'd have to consult a higher authority.

I separated Lulabelle from her favorite morning activity—grinding her big kitty-butt into Consort's pillow—and carried her to the back door:

QUINN: You want to go out?

Lulabelle arched and writhed in my arms.

LULABELLE: Woman, are you f**king insane?

Using my forehead as a springboard, she raced back to Consort's pillow. I shouted to Daughter, "Get the boots, it's going to rain."

I've learned to never doubt the cat. Her weather-wisdom is mysterious, deep and unfailing. Then again, if something nearly killed me, I'd get pretty smart about it, too.

Almost exactly four years ago this week, the forecast was for serious rain; days and days of it. El Niño was coming for an extended visit. Knowing how little she liked being wet, I encouraged our then-dog, Polly, to make one last bathroom trip late at night, before the rains came. Hearing the back door open, Lulabelle woke up, dashed from the couch to the back door and stared longingly into the dark.

"You don't want to go out tonight, Lu," I advised. "Big rain's coming."

Lulabelle sneered at me. "When I want your opinion," she seemed to say, "I'll tell you what it is. I'm outta here."

She darted off into the shadows, too excited about a night of mouse-hunting and other mayhem to even bother to slap Polly, teetering back towards the door. Within ninety minutes it started to rain. By midnight, it was torrential. By morning, there were foot-deep puddles on our street corner and a lap pool under the bay window. What there wasn't was a cat, nor was there a cat for the next seven days of nearly continuous downpour. I worried. Then I worried a lot. Then I grieved. Lu might not have had any respect for us as predatory mammals, but she liked us in a certain patronizing fashion and our kitty-stars weren't terrible. She'd have come home if she could. A house across the street had been tented for exterminating just before the rain began. It was all too easy to imagine that she had crawled under the house to escape the monsoon and been ...exterminated.

Two days after the rain stopped, I was walking out to the car with Daughter when we discovered Lulabelle sitting on our back doorstep. She was half of her usual size and couldn't put weight on her front paw, but she was home. We were ecstatic. The vet declared her remarkably healthy, quite underweight, and the owner of a sprained paw. A couple of days of rest and boiled chicken to convince her to eat again, and she was very nearly her old self.

Except for rain.

Lulabelle no longer does rain. There is no mouse so succulent, no bird so arrogant, no pug-being-walked-past-the-house-and-needing-a-smack-in-the-nose so tempting that it overrides her basic impulse to remain bone-dry for all eternity. Lulabelle seems to understand that she's used up several lifetimes' worth of luck, not to mention sebum, and that prudence is her best impulse going forward. For those of us who worried and cried for her when she was gone, this is both understandable and laudable. If there is any upside to her horrendous trial by precipitation — specifically, knowing whether or not we need to carry an umbrella today — well, that's just a bonus.

ME AGAINST THE WORLD

A while back, someone who comments here on occasion published an essay about how unbearably disgusting he found cats and, specifically, the cats of his two roommates. Apparently, there was a certain laissez-faire attitude towards litter-box maintenance and food-dish upkeep at his place. Even though I love cats, I certainly understood his revulsion, although I can make the argument that the cats weren't the slobs here, it was the owners who didn't take care of them properly. Part of me wanted to say, "Hey! Blame not the species. In fact, come to my house and you'll see how clean, neat and easy-going a properly-tended housecat can be."

Of course, at that exact moment, Lulabelle was peeing in the bathtub. And it wasn't the first time. After two days of shouting at her and curling my lip in contempt, I noted her urine had some blood in it. It seems Lu had developed a bladder infection. I recalled my mother telling me that Pooh, the cat I had growing up, would pee in the tub when she had a bladder infection. Whatever benefit tub-peeing provides the cat, it allows any human housemates to identify the problem; a problem which might go unnoticed in a regular litter box and most likely lead to more serious (and expensive) consequences. Tub-peeing is weird, and certainly not what anyone looks forward to first thing in the morning when all you want to do is to take a shower without having to break-out the Clorox, but no one can argue this behavior isn't effective. I whisked her in to the vet who prescribed antibiotics. Ten days later, she was fine. No more tub stuff.

Three weeks later, I was scrubbing the tub again. Another trip to the vet. Another round of antibiotics. This time, the vet massaged her torso in a seriously intrusive way, to see if he could feel kidney stones. "No kidney stones, just a really bad bladder infection," he declared. Having had bladder infections myself, and wincing in empathy at what must have felt like the doctor Rolfing her abdomen, I silently thanked Lulabelle for not killing him in the examination room.

That was two months ago. Early this week, I found Lulabelle slinking out of the bathroom, a place that — due to its abundant sources of water — is not her favorite hangout. Sure enough, the Wizzer of Odd had struck again. We went back to the vet, who was now puzzled. It turns out, cats have a predisposition towards bladder infection but it usually shows up in adolescence or as a consequence of old age. Lulabelle is in the prime of life. We decided to get her X-rayed to rule out a tiny yet vicious kidney stone. Minutes later, the tech brought Lu back into the examination room and set up a laptop with her X-ray image on it. Lu went back into her carrier and I waited for the vet to return. Standing there, my eyes were drawn to the glowing X-ray.

I always stare at test results in a doctor's office, which is adorable because I've never understood a single thing I'm looking at. It's like peering under the hood of a car: stuff and things, all very familiar and yet also very mysterious. But, darn it, this is my cat and I'm going to *participate*. At first, I allowed myself a certain pride that I could recognize vertebrae and a tail — two more things than I can usually identify in an X-ray. Peering at the image for a while, I became aware of something sharply anomalous in her upper abdomen. It was obviously solid and bone-like but nowhere near another bone. In fact, it was clearly suspended amid what trained doctor types would call "soft tissue". After years of peering fruitlessly at medical test results, I had every reason to believe I had finally diagnosed something. I was having my first *House* moment. I had found Lulabelle's kidney stone!

The vet came in, and leaned over the laptop, looking at the X-ray. A minute passed. Then another. I grew impatient. Couldn't he see what I had come to think of as *our* kidney stone? I was about to say something I hoped would sound coolly professional when he stated, "Well, she doesn't have kidney stones. Do you know how she got shot?"

She's...I...but...huh?

He pointed to my kidney stone and said, "That's a bullet."

I'll now summarize the next few minutes of my asking questions and spluttering. Lulabelle, at some point in the past, was shot with a very small-caliber weapon, possibly a pellet gun, probably from the back. It entered her backside and lodged in her pelvis, miraculously missing both her spine and major organs. Oddly enough, her bladder infection was completely unrelated. Still, had we not taken the X-ray, we'd never have known about this. Contrary to what I immediately assumed, my missing a bullet wound didn't make me the worst pet-owner in the world. The projectile was small. Its entry wound had been minimal and probably stopped bleeding quickly. In the several years we've owned her, Lu has spent more than one night away from home, not to mention the lost week of El Niño. It could have happened during any one of these sabbaticals and by the time she returned home she'd have stopped bleeding and her fur would have covered the scab. Or it may have happened one morning and scabbed over before she returned home that night. Or it could have happened before we owned her. If she knew, she wasn't telling. The vet saw no reason to remove the slug. He gave me a stronger antibiotic for her bladder infection and sent us on our way.

I drove home in silence for a few minutes and then called Consort to tell him the news. We both agreed that she was insanely lucky and we were grateful for that. I ranted for a few minutes about how certain humans probably needed a shooting or two themselves. Then I swung around to the thought that had been lurking at the back of my head for several minutes.

"Our cat Lulabelle, who takes pride in her killing skills, got shot on the street and walks around with a bullet in her, possibly for years. Should we change her name to Biggie Smalls? Fiddy? Tupac?"

Consort offered, "Lupac?"

So, as with so many of her urban compatriots, my cat now has her given name and her hood-name. May I present Lupac Shapurr.

UNDER MY THUMB

I've been told by certain well-meaning readers (actually, Consort) that it's a little too cat-centric around here lately and for this I apologize. If you're not an ailurophile, come back next week. I'll try to have run into something sharp or behaved in a socially questionable manner by then.

Three weeks ago, an urgent email request went out from the animal-rescue group where I volunteer. Someone had just dumped seven kittens at the doorstep and this being the peak of "kitten season", all the cages were full. Could people take cats? I quickly conferred with Consort—the unbelievably patient Consort—and offered to take one or two, but only on a temporary basis.

I went to the shelter and found the pen with the new arrivals. Some litters are affectionate. Some litters are playful. This bunch was fratricidal. If you've ever stumbled across cage-fighting on one of cable's higher channels, you've seen this litter. Sports drinks are missing a valuable sponsorship opportunity. I pointed to one ball of marauding, screaming fur and said, "We'll take that one."

The rolling ball was uncoiled and it turned out to be not one but two kittens. The volunteer held them arms-length apart but they continued to make stink-eyes at each other. I said feebly, "Should we get two who hate each other less?" and the volunteer laughed.

"These two *like* each other. Look at the runt," she said, pointing into the pen. One kitten, no longer than my thumb, was riding around on the head of his largest sibling, trying to give him a skull-skylight. Well, at least they were all healthy and attractive.

Because she's reading *Anne of Green Gables*, Daughter named one Anne and the other Diana. My suggestion of North Korea and South Korea was politely overridden, as was Hatfield & McCoy. As it turned out, the kittens are cloyingly affectionate towards anything that isn't another littermate. They catch my eye, they purr. Daughter talks to them and they knead her belly and bat their monstrous eyelashes. The dog gazes at them neutrally and they practically cavort. Then we all leave the room and they notice there's something else in the cage and the beatings commence. Later, I sneak into the laundry room and find them asleep across one another, sleeping deeply, a baby fang still sunk into an abdomen, a tiny, razor-sharp nail one millimeter away from a pulsing jugular.

After a couple of weeks, I decided that maybe the reason they kept trying to kill one another was because they were stuck in a smallish cage together, so I declared the entire laundry room their domain. This certainly improved their mood. It gave them many more places to hide behind and wait for the other one to walk by. Whatever the cat versions of "Ha-HA! We meet again!" and "No, Mr. Bond, I expect you to *die!* " are, I've heard them no fewer than sixteen times every day. But they seem pleased. And the laundry room floor is very nearly perfect for the countless ankle-wrenching little plastic toys they love to chase.

Then Lupac saunters in and they are enraptured.

[After discovering the bullet wedged in Lu's backside, I strongly advocated for her to be an indoor cat. Her negotiating position featured a unique counterproposal: the absolute refusal to ever use the litter box, choosing instead to take care of business in the middle of the kitchen floor. Lupac has since been grudgingly reassigned to indoor/outdoor status.]

For the first week, I would hustle Lupac from the back door to the kitchen, shepherding her trajectory through the laundry room like a PR flack assuring reporters that Ms. Shapurr would *love* to talk to them (and possibly murder them) if only she weren't running late for her appointment with stinky wet food. After a few days, I grew tired of this and started letting her move about unescorted. Lupac would strut in from the back yard, leap onto the dryer and eat her dinner. Anne and Diana would sit on the floor, watching her so closely and with such absorption they'd even stop trying to disembowel each another. It occurred to me that the kittens, without ever having seen her work, instinctively knew Lupac was the Real Deal. She carried on her a whiff of the outdoors, of things barely conceivable to the indoor cat, a life of excess and danger and dark pleasures. In sum, Lupac is Keith Richards to these kittens. She's a cigarette dangling from her lips and a skull ring away from going back on tour with Mick and the Boys.

For several days, they were respectful. She ignored them. But, as all Westerns have taught us, eventually someone will come gunning for the alpha. Two nights ago, Lupac, having finished her wet food, jumped down on to the floor and started to leave. Anne, the braver or possibly more stupid of the kittens, snuck up behind Lupac and placed her paw on Lu's tail.

The next few seconds passed as a series of glances. First, Anne looked to Diana, Diana looked to Anne. "Are you actually touching her tail?" "I am totally touching her tail." "I'm so impressed that I almost don't want to kill you right now."

Then, I looked at Anne and thought, "You aren't that dumb. *Krill* isn't that dumb. Take your paw off her tail, run for someplace small and pray to whatever God takes your calls that she's doesn't eat your skull." Anne looked at me in triumph. "I'm the boss of her!"

Finally, I looked at Lupac, who had already hit me with her cold, steady gaze. "Please," I implored her with my eyes. "Don't eat her. She's very young, it would be disturbing for me to watch and I think she's nearly all gristle." Lupac looked at me, meaningfully and silently and then, never looking at either of them, pulled her tail out from under Anne's paw, swung past her, strolled to the kittens' food bowl, ate all their wet food, mumbled something unintelligible under her breath and walked towards the door. At the door, she took a second to whack one of the baby's toys backwards. It hit Anne squarely between the eyes.

The kittens stayed frozen in awe for at least a minute. I suspect this is just how Keith would have handled it.

DOCTOR, DOCTOR. GIMME THE NEWS

Some days, you find the adventure. Some days, the adventure finds you. One day, I'm watching my daughter power down mochi for breakfast, the next day I'm staring at a cat's armpit.

Actually, I was staring at a cat's armpit at night, which is part of the problem. I've already mentioned that Consort is a night owl but I don't think I've stressed exactly how much of a morning-person I am. It's not as if I insist the pre-dawn hours are the most productive of the day — at least partially because I'm not certain I *have* productive hours of the day — but I do function best during daylight. In fact, an ex nicknamed me *Parakeet*. He swore if you threw a black cloth over my head I'd think it was nighttime and fall instantly to sleep. And that was back in my twenties, before a child, an old house and general wear-and-tear took their toll. Nowadays, I can't do Sudoku after five p.m., I can't operate an iPhone after seven p.m. and I can't wield a stain-removing crayon after eight-thirty. By eleven o'clock, I'm furniture that whines.

So last night at ten o'clock, I was sitting at the kitchen table girding my loins for another routine trek to the bedroom when I heard Lupac pounding against the back door. Finally, my liege was home. She was three hours later than usual but she would spend the night inside. I stumbled to the back door and let her in. She raced past me and leapt up to her food bowl on the laundry counter. The instant she flew past, my brain offered up the word "pink." I waited to see if this meant something while, out of habit, I closed and locked the door. My brain, sighing at its workload, snapped a bit louder: "Pink! On the cat!" Let's all remember, Lu is a black cat, so the last employee working in my brain for the night wanted me to know this was not normal. I shuffled over to the counter and gazed listlessly upon the cat. There, in what would have been her armpit had she possessed arms, was a gaping pink wound the size of a quarter.

I triaged her to the best of my ability. The wound was open, but not bleeding. If her relationship with the food dish was any indication, her appetite was fine. Touching around the injury grossed me out but didn't seem to bother her at all. I summoned Consort. Together, we stared at the wound while the cat finished off her dinner. Did she need to go to the ER tonight or could we wait until morning and see her regular vet? Consort deferred to me — I'm the one who had pets her entire life, he was a rank amateur. Still, by this point in the evening, my brain had been replaced by a Brillo pad and some socks so this level of decision-making was taxing my abilities. I phoned the head of our rescue group and gave her the details. Kindly, she didn't bark at me for calling her at ten-thirty but instead reminded me how quickly a feral cat's bite, if it was that, can go septic. By morning, Lu could be dying from an infection. Right. Off to the vet. Now I just had to remember how to tie my shoes. Consort offered to take the cat but my steel wool and sock-filled cranium rallied and I made a compelling argument for this being my responsibility and not his. This stunned Consort into acquiescence, possibly because it was the most coherent thing I'd said after nightfall in many years. Gingerly, we wedged Lupac into a carrier and I headed off to the pet Emergency Room.

The pet ER was empty, and I was glad. This meant that we'd be seen before I lost the power of human speech. Also, a pet emergency room is a God-awful place, worse even than a human emergency room. Having spent too much time in both, I can assure you that sometimes in a human ER, you get a patient in labor, which makes everyone kind of excited and happy; and sometimes you get an especially entertaining un-medicated psych patient or a fascinating crime-related drama unfolds. In the pet Emergency Room, all you get is despair. You aren't sitting there in the middle of the night with your beloved pet because he was looking a bit peaked. Usually someone is covered in pet-blood, another person is sobbing helplessly and a third person is shouting into a cell-phone "Just get down here now if you want to say goodbye to Mr. Whiskers!" An empty waiting room was good. I filled out paperwork. I got to the part about preexisting conditions and confidently wrote down that she'd had a steroid shot two weeks before because she has granuloma. I handed in the paperwork and the cat. The woman took both and came back out again.

"Granuloma?" The woman asked. "The doctor wants to know if you mean Eosinophilic Granuloma?"

Sure, that one. I was pleased that I had remembered the granuloma, and also how to touch my thumb to my forefinger. The woman seemed unimpressed. A few minutes passed. The gym sock stirred slightly in my skull.

"Did I write down that she has chronic bladder infections?"

We checked the record. I had not. I scribbled it in. I picked up a *Details* magazine from 2003. A few more minutes passed. The scouring pad tossed up another fact.

"Do you need to know she has a heart murmur?"

Again, the paperwork came out. I smiled in a friendly way at the receptionist. Perhaps it was a trick of the light, but she appeared to sneer. I scribbled in the heart murmur and sat back down. My eye fell upon a *TV Guide* crossword puzzle: "Television Host _____ Seacrest." Four letters. I struggled over that one. Suddenly, I remember something.

"Do you need to know that she has a bullet in her pelvis?"

"Being as she's going to have X-rays, *yes*."

Night owls are snotty.

At 1:45, I handed over my credit card to cover the down-payment for the repairs to Lu's armpit. I could come back and get her in the morning, but no later than 7:30 because that's when they closed and she'd be stuck there for the next day at great expense. Because I was home twenty minutes later, I'm guessing I drove, but I can't account for it. If I went into the bedroom I'd probably wake up Consort, who may or may not have just gone to sleep, so I lay down on the couch and pulled a blanket over me, enjoying the darkness and the quiet and the absence of veterinary sneering. My inner parakeet was pleased. Then, the foster-kittens ran in. They are now almost four months old and just about the most darling, wonderful girls on earth during the day. At night, however, they are Thing One and Thing Two, the Merry Mistresses of Mayhem. My sleeping on the couch was, apparently, Christmas come early for them. I became feline Pilates equipment for the entire night.

It turns out that I only like early mornings when I haven't been awake for most of the previous night. Seven o'clock attacked me like a hung-over wolverine. I crawled to the kitchen and made myself the tea version of a double-espresso: green tea so thick it looked like a fairway at Augusta. I drove carefully back to the ER and paid more ransom to spring my cat. The doctor showed me the wound, now neatly sewn shut. The bottle of antibiotics to be given for the next ten days thrilled neither of us. They had shaved the bottom half of her front leg to insert an IV and then, for unknown reasons, shaved the other front leg as well. With her nearly globular shape, threatening expression and shaved skinny ankles, she resembled the would-be gangsters I sometimes saw in east LA, with their oversized manpris and incongruously tiny calves covered in white socks. As with the bangers, I kept my snarky fashion commentary to myself.

We got to the car. I put Lu's crate in the back seat and glanced down at her. She rewarded me with an epic yawn. I'm guessing she didn't have the night she had planned either. I scritched her head through the grating and said, "Lu, let's get home and take a nice nap."

And so we did.

SHEPHERDS QUAKE AT THE SIGHT

You have family due in six hours and they just called from the airport to let you know Cousin Margaret is also bringing her Shih Tzu and your nephew's new wife will need vegan options at the dinner table.

Shhh, let it out.

All your daughter wants is that stupid hamster toy that is so popular even NPR did a story on it, and you swore to get it even though another mom told you it was made of enriched uranium and the vestigial organs of Chinese prisoners. You have been covertly texting a teenager who works at a nearby toy store, offering him up to five times face value for an object you suspect will be adored by its new owner for about seven hours.

I know, I know.

It's been twelve days since the first day of Chanukah and your entire house still smells of potato pancakes and you just found a holiday gelt in the dryer with the white towels?

You don't remember seeing the cat eat tinsel but the litter-box now looks like a revolting fireworks display?

You just remembered you have godchildren in Sumatra who will be expecting something thoughtful from you in forty-eight hours?

Scrooge had Christmases Past, Present and Future to put things in perspective. You have Christmas Quinn. So grab a glass of strongly-spiked something and come to my house.

First, come to the living room. That lump on the couch, under the quilts? That's my daughter. She's celebrating the holiday season by having a stomach virus. It arrived Monday night, halfway through a fancy holiday dinner at a very nice restaurant with my mother. Nothing says holiday quite like a child informing you if you don't move the cheese soufflé she's going to hurl all over grandma's Yorkshire pudding. Over the past thirty-six hours, she's eaten three garbanzo beans, six water-crackers and a chip. We've passed this time, ordinarily spent watching her eat, listening instead to the moment-to-moment pathology of her ailment. It's a mild bug, but it's a chatty one.

Next to the quilted lump lecturing about vomit is a Christmas tree. It's a very nice Christmas tree. Big and piney. Next to the Christmas tree is a spray-bottle. There is a spray-bottle because we have a pair of six month-old, foster kittens — Anne and Diana, a.k.a. *Thing One* and *Thing Two*. If you've had a Christmas tree and kittens, I need say no more. If you haven't, I'll try to explain it from their perspective. Imagine something you've always wanted, covered in other things that tempt and call out to your very soul. [For me this would be runway-thin thighs, a pile of unread *Vanity Fair* magazines, and salted caramels.] Now, imagine that every time you got near this venerated object, a looming, omniscient beast shouted "NO!" and your face was suddenly splashed with vile liquid. This is Christmas with a kitten. We have two.

What we don't have is an adult cat. Two weeks ago, Lupac took off for her usual day of hunting and sneering, and has yet to return. She'd been gone for a week before, but never two. She's micro-chipped and she has a solid collar. If any cat could disappear for six months and then return home with a tattoo and an enigmatic expression, it's my Lupac, but a recurring motif of this past week is me standing at the back door, looking miserable, and shouting to the moon about soy turkey. Any future memory of this Christmas will include a visual of me nostalgically holding a bag of dry-food specifically formulated for cats with chronic bladder problems. Lupac's mysterious absence is part of the reason I'm keeping the kittens over the holidays. The kid and I need a small, weird mammal or two around. I mean, besides each other. Consort, in his saintly way, quietly upped his Azelastine prescription.

In the dining room, there is the gingerbread house. Please don't touch that. The only thing holding it together is gumdrops and several cans of kidney beans hidden within. During construction, a load-bearing wall cracked and its entire north side has been bulging ominously for days. Who knew kidney beans were the flying buttresses of holiday architecture? Thanks to everyone who wrote in and said

"Quinn, gingerbread houses don't need to be nearly as sturdy as you're making them." Because of you, next year the kid and I will create a candy house that suggests the Seventh Ward after Katrina with renewed confidence.

Here's the kitchen, and here's the pumpkin bread. And here's more pumpkin bread. And here. And also here. It's the one thing I make every year. It's the only thing I make every year. One loaf is left for the house. I sliced into one. Unbeknownst to me, Consort sliced into another one. At some point before the first of many discussions about barfing up Beef Wellington, the kid sliced into one. So we now have three pumpkin breads to give away and three for us. I'm encouraging Consort to make sandwiches with it. And French toast. And attic insulation. I'm assigning one thinly sliced loaf for creative gift-wrapping. I'm flinging bits of it at the kittens when they lunge towards the tree. I'm very tired of pumpkin bread.

Next to one loaf, there are Christmas cards, unsigned and unsent. We're not sending out Christmas cards this year. We allowed ourselves one day in which to get the annual holiday photograph of the kid. She was going to be dressed up anyway, hair done, nice shoes, and we'd be someplace with gorgeous backgrounds and lovely light. The shortened winter day ended up giving us twelve minutes to get the picture during which time Consort took seven shots, six of which captured Daughter doing something odd with her eyelid. The gothic stone background, so promising in daylight, resembled the exercise yard of a state prison once the sun went down. By the time I realized we needed to take another photo, it was the December twentieth. The next day, she took to the couch, too green to stand, much less pose. I'm toying with starting a new tradition: President's Day cards.

And here's the garage. And here's the storage shed behind the garage. And here inside the storage shed is where Christmas presents hide out before their official debut. Before she took to the couch for an interlude of emesis and medical dictation, my daughter snooped. We stow Christmas presents in the storage shed not simply because it has a lock — I believe my daughter would learn lock picking from felony.com if she could discover whether or not she's getting fashionable leg-warmers this year. No, we keep the Christmas presents in here because once, when she accompanied her dad to the shed to retrieve a wheelbarrow, she saw a spider the size of a pluot and has never been back since. Her love for all living creatures doesn't extend to spiders. Daughter is the only child I know who cheers at the end of *Charlotte's Web*. I'd try to raise her awareness of the wonderful utility of spiders, but since they are acting as my bouncers, I see no need to make them less alarming just yet.

See, doesn't my life put the Holiday Season into perspective? I had a book published this year. Naively, I expected a published author would have a more attractive Christmas. Dan Brown might own a spray-bottle, but I doubt he's decorating around it. But it's the end of the year and while my work is now on a different shelf, I'm still me. I'm still delighted by my kid, amused by my pets, horrified by my house and devoted to my guy. And readers, I'm so very grateful to you all. Your comments give me laughs and thoughts and windows into worlds I don't even have to put on shoes to enter. Writing these posts fulfills me, but hearing from you makes me buoyant. Have a peaceful and prosperous New Year.

And take a slice of pumpkin bread with you for the road.

NEVER WERE THERE SUCH
DEVOTED SISTERS

Finally! Quinn the slacker rouses from her winter hibernation and sets paws to keyboard. If guilt were writing, I'd have posted this entry days ago. Then again, if guilt were writing, I'd match the output of the Russian masters, word-for-word, on a daily basis.

To answer the inevitable first question: no, Lu the cat hasn't come home. I can only hope someone sees her tag or scans her for a chip and she comes back to us somehow, but I'm keeping my expectations realistic. Oddly enough, we haven't seen Victor/Victoria around either since Lu went missing. Victor/Victoria is an ovoid tabby of unknown gender who spent mornings in our front yard and whom Lu appeared to like, which is to say didn't try to eviscerate. Daughter suggested they ran off to get married. Consort suggested Lu and Victor/Victoria bought an RV and moved to Branson, Missouri, where they could live unnoticed because so many people there are similarly shaped. I doubt this. Lu doesn't strike me as a fan of The Oak Ridge Boys.

Nevertheless, she's gone to her next adventure and wherever she is, we love her and we hope she's raising hell.

Luckily for me—the parent not looking forward to a grieving child pining for her fur-football-with-fishbreath sister —we have the foster kittens to distract us. For the past four years we've fostered kittens, usually during "kitten season" when the shelters tend to overflow with new issue. Every year, someone would see us enjoying the endless kitten-y silliness and announce "You're keeping this one" and I'd always explain that no, tiny kittens are great fun to have around but our job was to keep them safe and happy and get them ready for their full-time family. Anne and Diana were just another couple of gears in this great, adopt-a-cat engine.

But no one told *them* that.

At first, we started letting them out beyond the laundry room, mostly because we didn't have any choice with them adhering like a burr to any mammal that passed through. They still had to spend nights in there, though. That was the rule. Within days, Diana, the fluffy tortoise kitten, wouldn't sleep anywhere but nestled in the kid's armpit, kneading the sleeve of her pajama top. Anne, the ginger tabby, favored me, mostly when I was trying to work. Sensing an unspoken need, she'd spring neatly into my lap and commence reducing the thread count of my pants. Both girls wake up for their evening workout just about the time I go to bed, which is five minutes before Consort starts his evening television ritual of watching all the channels at once. One morning over coffee, Consort told me about the previous night, when he'd stumbled across a Harrison Ford movie about...something.

You know, average man, armed only with superior intellect, some FBI training and a thrilling score, does mano-a-mano battle with sadistic, evil guy who is usually kind of British. I don't know. A Harrison Ford movie.

Anyway, Consort hadn't seen this one before and, against his will, he got drawn in, even though it was on basic cable and a commercial popped up every three minutes or so. Fully awake, the kittens galloped through the room bent on mayhem. Hours later, the movie finally reached the dramatic peak: evil sort-of British guy and Harrison faced off, a couple of more commercial breaks happened, and then, finally, the big fight scene starte—

The screen went black. The kittens had been wrestling behind the TV and somehow unplugged it.

By the time he got the TV back on, there was another commercial. When that ended, Harrison, blood-flecked and triumphant, was reuniting with his family. Consort never got to experience his macho-movie climax. An axe may have been involved. And a skull. But he missed it. The kittens had completely ruined the cathartic payoff of a 90-minute movie stretched to three hours by the miracle of basic cable. And yet Consort didn't strangle them. In fact, he was laughing as he told the story. We loved these critters. They were going to make someone great pets. They were great cats.

But apparently not on weekends. And especially not when they were being shown to potential adoptive families at the shelter. There, they would huddle together at the back of their cage, glaring and hissing at potential adopters, making noises as if they'd been found living behind Chernobyl. I came to pick them up one Sunday night and the woman who runs the place was crawling around under a bookcase. It seems Anne had sprung herself from the cage, raced under the bottom shelf and was batting at anyone who got near her. The rescue leader, usually an unflappable presence when it comes to cats, was flapped. This little monster would not come out.

I leaned over and said, "Anne, pumpkin, I'm here. Let's go home." She shot out from under the bookshelf like a cannonball, landing somewhere on my abdomen and latching on with all four paws. The rescue-group leader said, "We need to get them out of your house. They're already so devoted to each other they'll have to be adopted together. And now they're getting that attached to you."

I agreed. In theory. I also begged for one more week with them because...I don't know, they'd get *less* devoted to us after spending more time together? It seemed possible; people have gotten tired of me in a week. That week passed, and then another, during which Lu left. By this point, we couldn't possibly send them back during the week and it didn't make much sense to send them for the weekend showings because they made such a dreadful first impression. And then, late one night, I went in to check on the kid and straighten her blankets. I found Anne sprawled around the kid's feet sound asleep and Diana under the covers, kneading the duvet. That's when I realized: sometimes the family you get them ready for is your own.

I Swiffer more now than I used to. I bathe them in Allerpet. They don't go outside, nor will they, which should keep the allergens slightly less abundant. The air purifier runs 24/7. Consort is a saint and I'm very grateful for him. I'm also grateful for the insistent lump of orange presence currently purring in my lap as I write this, reminding me once again that in life, the unexpected can be pretty horrible. But it can also be pretty wonderful.

YOU'VE READ OF SEVERAL KINDS
OF CAT

"But," I can hear a percentage of my readers say in increasingly plangent tones. "What about the new kittens?"

Well, Cat People, the kittens are fine. They are now half-grown girls, being of great length and some width and having had their Very Special Operation. Their names are still Anne and Diana, which made more sense when they were only staying a month or so. Anne and DiANA are entirely too similar for ease of differentiation. Usually, we just say "Annandiana," as if they're conjoined. Consort avoids the whole situation by referring to both cats as "He."

I kept waiting to write about them when their shadow-side appeared, figuring it made for better writing. Also, having lived with Lulabelle lo these many years, I assumed they'd be nothing but a shadow side, with briefs shafts of psychic light between the dark clouds of mouse-death. But these girls are so darling it almost cloys. They wear doll dresses without complaint. They not only consent to being carried around like babies, they purr while it's happening. Each one chases her own tail. After their first murderous weeks together, they love each other now with obvious, uninhibited joy; if they could, they'd braid each other's ears. After having lived for many years with the cat version of Marianne Faithfull (the heroin years), I'm now roomies with Vanessa Hudgens (the *High School Musical* years). Which is how I finally came to give them their first nickname:

Readers, may I present...the Ingénues.

All round cheeks, round eyes and perfectly clean little paws, their greatest goal in life is twenty minutes bossing around the felt mouse, followed by the cooing adoration of their human big sister. I didn't know Lu well when she was their age, but I can guarantee she had already felt the singular joy of a bird's neck snapping in her capable maw. The Ingénues are like those kids who believe hamburger meat grows at the grocery store. They are no more allowed to go outside than the star of a Disney Channel sitcom would be left on the interstate to hitch her way home. My job with Lupac was to keep her inside often enough so the local fauna could replenish itself. My job with the Ingénues is to protect their innocence.

They have exactly one oddity. At 10:30 every night, on the dot, they race around the house very, very quickly. If it weren't so adorable, this behavior would be deemed *frantic*. But they are, so it's not. Then, having warmed up for a few minutes, they stare fixedly at a spot on the wall and jump at it for about half an hour. Did I mention this spot is visible only to them and is about five feet off the ground?

So what about the new kittens? They're very sweet. They're loud. They're strange, but punctually strange. And they're home.

IN MY ROOM

This morning I was Swiffering the house—specifically, our bedroom—because it's spring and because we have entirely too many pets whose goal in life is to "shed until bald." This meant I was doing something that involved movement, which also meant the two tween-aged cats had to supervise the activity and occasionally swat at the Swiffer.

[I just noticed "Swat the Swiffer" sounds like a code-phrase for one of those things usually done in private, but I can't decide which. If you feel so inclined, decide which private act it describes and then use the phrase freely.]

Since the whole point of Swiffering was to reduce the amount of animal hair in the bedroom, all this leaping and pouncing, which was creating a fresh batch of fur-tumbleweeds, struck me as counterproductive. The cats needed to leave. They sensed I wanted them to leave so they jetéd under the furniture and as far back against the wall as they could, first under the headboard, then under the dresser.

I flailed at them first with my hands, then with my arms and finally with the Swiffer, which must have seemed like being accosted by a squat, rectangular, ferret. Were I under there, I would have taken this aggressive behavior as a specific and very compelling motivation to leave the room. But I am not a cat. What the cats took from these incursions was: "Get further into the room. Find better places to hide. Hunker down. Under no circumstance leave this room."

Fifteen minutes. Fifteen minutes of leaping, dashing, juking, feinting, and sliding across the floor. That was me. The cats danced in a precise and orderly fashion from one shadowy nook to another, shedding one-third their fur inventory with each migration. In one heart-stopping moment, Diana's evasive maneuvers found her near the bedroom door where I lunged in an acrobatic yet ultimately foiled effort to shoo her all the way out. This new level of wrangling and counter-wrangling caused her to shed a heretofore-undiscovered layer of fur. It also caught the dog's attention, so he wandered in and shed for a minute or so himself until I shoved him outside with my leg.

Finally, I flung myself under the bureau, blindly grabbed a leg and a hank of fur and pulled, hoping to God it was a cat. Under the bureau one never knows. It was a cat and I sent her on her way into the house. A minute later, I snagged the other one and jettisoned her as well. They stood in the hallway for a second staring at nothing in particular, possibly stunned, possibly enjoying a life of utter indifference once again. The morning sun hit them in such a way that I was able to enjoy the full effect of the nimbus of fur and dander circling them like a dusty halo. It floated up and away from each of them like an aura, caught the faint current of morning breeze in the hallway...and wafted straight back into the bedroom.

BUT THEY'RE COUSINS, IDENTICAL COUSINS ALL THE WAY

The ingénue-cats have earned a new nickname: they are *The Causins*. Yes, I can spell. And, yes, I'm pretty certain they were sibling littermates. They're *The Causins* because there is no better explanation for anything they do besides: 'Cause.

Why is Diana eating the side of the bed? 'Cause.

Why did Anne wedge herself between a half-open window sash and its screen, which triggered a claustrophobic panic requiring two adults, power tools and fifteen minutes to disengage her? 'Cause.

Why did Diana jump up and down in an empty corner like a gymnast for twenty minutes this morning, then rush into Daughter's room, grab a sock and trot around the house with it like an Olympic medalist? 'Cause.

Why did Anne start walking behind me for minutes at a time, telling me the entire story of her life? 'Cause. [But it does explain why Anne is now referred to as Squeakers.]

Why did one of them eat a Band-Aid and then discover a Band-Aid isn't food? And why did the mystery cat learn this lesson on my only suede purse? You guessed it: 'Cause.

Lupac came to us as an adult cat. Had she been human, she would have been a dour workaholic who spent her rare off-work hours flipping through feline trade magazines such as *Small Prey Monthly* or *Professional Dog Smacking.* Lu's fun—the fun of playing with thumb-sized things until they exsanguinated—was the feline version of single-malt Scotch. It was an unadorned, adult kind of fun. It was Amish fun.

I had forgotten that before they become adult cats dozing in the sun, dreaming of a chewy mouse liver, they are youthful semi-kittens, behaving like lunatics. Squeakers and Diana march to the beat of their own drummer, only it's less a march than a dash. And it's not so much a drum as a kazoo. And because they're indoor cats and will remain so forever, I am haunted by the premonition that they will be doing inexplicable things for years. I can put Bitter Apple on the bedposts to keep them from chewing it but that just means they'll knock a jar of expensive black olives down from the cabinet and sneeze on it.

But they are attractive and sweet and I forgive them for being young and exuberant. They are my trophy wives, off to change their hair color, or get to a yoga class, or shove all their toys under the bureau. And I am their sugar daddy, fondly admiring their good looks and lively schedule, and seizing whatever opportunities I get to rest when they aren't around.

THE MYSTICAL DIVINITY OF UNASHAMED FELINITY

After several heart-stopping moments recently, I have come to a powerful realization. Cat toys, which have become favored by cats and therefore moved from location to location throughout the house, take one of two forms:

1. They look exactly like something once living and now dead (especially if spotted out of the corner of your eye).

2. They feel exactly like something once living and now dead (especially if discovered under your instep when you get up to go to the bathroom and the room is dark and you aren't terribly clear-minded).

I'm off to drink chamomile tea now.

BABY, IT'S COLD OUTSIDE

We had a houseguest for two weeks. Our house is small and space is limited so it's not a place for extended company, but he was a remarkably easy guest. He stayed in his room. He was very quiet. He didn't object to our watching "Sons of Anarchy." He even brought his own special food because he's on a special diet though, in truth, I could have done without finding a jar of mealworms in my fridge every morning.

It began, as everything modern does, with an email. "Can Cyril stay with you?" Our friends, Robin and her family, were heading out of town for two weeks and their regular lizard-sitter dropped out at the last minute. Perhaps he'd received a more glamorous offer, perhaps involving a Gila monster. In any case, I gladly offered my home and an hour later, Cyril arrived. He had a large rectangular terrarium, a water bowl, a food bowl, a big stick for lizarding on, a screen-mesh lid to repel intruders (such as cats), and a heating lamp. We placed him in the laundry room, the place with the largest unused table. I was handed the jar of mealworms and told to feed him every three days or so. "If you forget to feed him for a couple of days," Robin explained, adjusting the heat lamp over his stick, "Don't worry, he'll be fine. He'll just bite you when you put in his worms. But he doesn't have any teeth."

Daughter, having been excited at the idea of a new pet, grew instantly indifferent when confronted with food that wriggled, as live worms tend to do, and with the plausible threat of punitive lizard biting, however toothless. Cyril sat on his lizarding stick and squinted at me with one ball-bearing eye. I made a silent vow not to let it get that far.

Over the next few days, I learned how little effort it requires to micromanage a reptile. I'd look into his cage and notice he had kicked some sand into his water so I'd carefully clean the bowl and freshen the water. Ten minutes later the water was a sand-colored slurry just like before. I would clean out rice-sized extrusions of lizard dung but an hour later, I'd walk by and notice a poop grain exactly where I had removed the last one. It seems that: a) Cyril knew exactly how he wanted things to be, and b) I was actively ruining his chances to make the cover of *Lézard Decor*. What most amazed me was how he completed all his domestic chores without my once ever seeing him move. Every time I checked in on him, he was resting on the lizarding stick, crouching under the lizarding stick or sitting next to the lizarding stick, practicing his inscrutable gaze into the middle distance; but I never actually saw him *move* to any of these locations. Not once. Every third day, I'd pick out the fattest mealworms and deliver his supper. Every fourth day, the mealworms would be gone and the lizard would be exactly where I'd last seen him, motionless, on his stick, nowhere near the food or the carefully situated, rice-sized poop. Like a few people I've met over the years, Cyril was mystifying without actually being interesting.

On day six, I came into the laundry room and discovered Squeakers sitting on the screen on top of the cage. She stared in rapt, tiger-like fascination down at the lizard. Cyril, showing more interest in her than he ever showed in me, his domestic servant, stared back up at Squee, equally motionless. The mesh, which was meant to separate them, bowed downward ominously. I shrieked, dashed in and removed the cat from the room. But this bell had been rung. The Ingénues now knew there was something in the house that was very, very interesting. It awakened some part of their feral brains [okay, sure, their lizard-brains]. It was the part that told them: *You know, food doesn't always come from the impossible-to-open storage bin next to the dryer. Sometimes, food is a wonderful game.*

Initially, I tried to keep them out of the laundry room altogether but this was their turf, they knew all its secret portals and hidden stairways. I tried putting a towel over the cage to help them forget. No dice. Unless I planned to spend the next fifteen days as a reptile's twenty-four hour bodyguard, I needed to find Cyril a safer place to live. So, we moved him into the garage. The cats never went out there so he'd be safe. The only downside was that it gets pretty hot in the garage this time of year. Then again, Cyril was a desert creature who traveled with his own heat lamp. I assumed spending two weeks in a hot garage would, for a lizard, be like a spa retreat. Cyril would be warm and safe and I wouldn't be required to tell a wonderful friend that my cat ate her lizard. All would be well.

I don't know how much meteorology you follow but a couple of weeks ago we had a real heat wave out here.

For several peak days of the heat wave, Cyril certainly didn't need his heat lamp. Every hour or so, I checked his cage thermometer; if it was over 100 degrees, I'd open the garage door and hang out with him until it was under 100 degrees again. I added an ice cube to his dish, to create cool fresh water. He sat on his lizarding stick and tried his best to pretend he was alone, never so much as glancing at me. I now have some sense of what it will be like to take Daughter to the mall when she's fifteen.

Finally, the heat broke. And then it broke further, and then a little further still. A week to the day after we recorded a temperature of 104 degrees, it fell to 60 degrees and raining. We won't even discuss my wardrobe issues. I now had responsibility for a lizard that needed his cage to stay at 80 degrees living in an outbuilding with no heat and no insulation. My trips the garage to make sure he wasn't turning into lizard jerky now became trips to make sure he wasn't a frozen lizard popsicle. I kept the heat lamp on all the time now, its red glow reminiscent of a catering table, but I worried that leaving it on all night would generate insufficient warmth and turn Cyril's cage into a sort of lizard Abu Ghraib. One afternoon, I finally lugged the terrarium back into the laundry room but within minutes I found Squeakers curling around its glass walls, staring in fascination at this new blinking chew toy. Out Cyril went again, back to the garage. On went the heat lamp. I whispered, "I'm so sorry" to the lizard that huddled under his lizarding stick and gazed back at me phlegmatically. I obsessed about whether lizards experienced a REM cycle and what quality of life they'd have if deprived of it.

This Thursday morning, my friend's husband called. They were back from their trip and would swing by in about an hour to pick up Cyril. I pranced out to the garage to let Cyril know his family was coming to get him and froze in my tracks. The heat lamp was off. Then I remembered that it had been hot in the garage the day before and I decided to give him a couple of hours of semi-darkness before turning it back on for the night. Only I had never remembered to come back out and turn it on. Fearfully, I tiptoed to the cage. Cyril was under the lizarding stick, unresponsive. This wasn't surprising, as I had never actually seen Cyril in a state I'd call *responsive*, but this seemed even less responsive than usual. I opened the lid and poked him. Then I prodded him. Then I tipped him over, his little legs locked in stiff imitation of his lizarding stick. He had all the animation of a kitchen utensil. Great. I had taken good care of Cyril for two weeks and managed to *kill him in the final eight hours?*

Then, my favorite medical saying came to mind: "You're not dead until you're warm and dead."

I hauled Cyril's cage and heat lamp back into the laundry room and whispered to him to walk away from the light and back towards us. Not that I wanted a warm, dead lizard in my house; but if children can fall into freezing-cold rivers, exist without a pulse for an hour or more, and still be revived without neurological damage, I was going to bake myself a lizard and hope for the best. I turned the heat lamp on and wrapped the cage in a towel, both to hold in the heat and dissuade the cats. After ten minutes, I unwrapped the towel. He was still on his back, but his legs seemed less rigid. Another twenty minutes, another towel unwrapping. Now, he was on his feet again. Ten minutes after that, he was at the top of his lizarding stick, getting as close to the heat lamp as possible. I might quibble that it would have been nice to see him actually, you know...move. But I was deeply grateful that he wasn't, you know... dead.

My friend's husband arrived minutes later with the kids. We collected the terrarium from the laundry room and the mealworms from the fridge. Having sworn to myself I wasn't going to say anything, I promptly whispered the entire story to the father as our children threatened each other with mealworms.

"Would have been fine by me," he said, looking bleakly at Cyril. "Robin, too. We never thought he'd last this long. I'm sure Jack (their youngest) would have been upset, so it worked out for the best, I guess." Then he smiled ever so slightly, imagining, I'm sure, a lizard-free lifestyle. "Of course," he added, as he slammed the tailgate shut, "We just would have blamed it on you."

They all thanked me sincerely for taking such good care of Cyril. I thanked Cyril for somehow surviving my care. They drove off. I went inside to have a midday lie-down on my lizarding stick.

HOPPIN' DOWN THE BUNNY
TRAIL

In my childhood, one of my nicknames was Saint Francis.

We weren't Catholic. I rarely wore brown robes. I earned this nickname because animals flocked around me, especially the ones who weren't entirely certain whom to call "Mom" or "Can-opener." This wasn't something I cultivated with any specific behavior on my part but it happened all the time and it's still the case.

When I visit an outdoor cafe, stray puppies nose under my table, and *only* my table. Feral cats jump into my car when I'm washing it in the driveway. Strangers walk up to me in the street holding out a paper bag and say, "I'm moving to Guam, do you want this hamster?" Think I'm exaggerating? After one of my readings for *Notes from the Underwire*, the bookstore set up a folding table in an outside patio for me to greet fans and sign books. I was happily greeting and signing when I felt a "whoosh" past my face and then a small "thump" in my lap. I looked down to see a baby bird, clearly taking his first flight out of the nest, pulled into the gravitational field of my animal magnetism. The bird was startled. I wasn't.

Last Sunday, I was taking a stroll around the neighborhood when I spotted a couple and their small daughter. The parents were chasing after their toddler, a giggling pixie in hot pursuit of a roundish stone on someone's yard. Upon closer inspection, I saw the stone was, in fact, a domesticated rabbit. The baby got close and shrieked in delight. The rabbit continued eating clover shoots in a perfectly rabbit sort of way. Eventually, the family continued on their walk but I inched closer to check out the bunny. This was definitely a bunny, as opposed to a wild rabbit. It allowed me to get within a foot or so of it before bounding off towards more grass. It eyed me neutrally. I said aloud, "You take care of yourself, little rabbit." This was not possible, of course. Domesticated rabbits on the streets last until they don't. Something eats them, or something hits them. I'm not happy about this, but it wasn't in my yard and it wasn't my responsibility. Honesty demands that I admit to feeling nothing but relief over that. I went on my merry way.

Yesterday morning, I had to do someone a favor. I mention this not because I need your admiration, but because it was a boring, demanding favor and I returned home in a "Well, *I'm* certainly eating carbs and putting Quinn first for the rest of today" sort of mood. So you will imagine my first reaction when I saw the same rabbit from last weekend on my front steps. And you'll certainly understand my dismay when the rabbit, upon seeing me, hopped directly towards me with a singular purpose.

Rabbits can't convey much by way of the more subtle emotional states but this encounter seemed like a reunion of family members separated by war. He hopped directly onto my foot and sat there in what appeared to be utter delight. I tentatively touched his ear. He rolled over onto my ankle and nuzzled my instep. He had travelled three blocks and crossed a busy street to sit in my yard and make me swear.

Let me sum up the next hour: Get cat carrier. Fill cat carrier with rabbit. Go to rescue group. It's a boy! My, it certainly is a boy, isn't it? Get greens from rescue group. Get hay from rescue group. Get in car. Take Benadryl. Go home. Set up temporary cage. Take digital snapshot for pleading email and flyers. Send pleading email. Print flyers. Take more Benadryl. Recently, I've been told I'm not allergic to rabbits but to hay. However, since it's not a rabbit without hay, and since even touching the rabbit and then unconsciously flicking my bangs back caused a red itchy welt on my forehead, it's safe to say this story isn't going to end with "Oh, what the hell. Let's keep him." So he can't stay.

But neither can he go.

The rescue group I work with is licensed to have no more than six rabbits. We have six rabbits. All rabbit-rescue groups are full. If I put him in the city shelter he'll be dead in a week. I have no room for this. I'm writing another book. I'm home-schooling my daughter. I'm considering buying nicer towels. And now, it would appear, I'm keeping a rabbit for a week to see if someone puts up a "Lost Rabbit" flyer. Or responds to my "Found Rabbit" flyer. Or my email. Or the local word-of-mouth critter network. Either way, I'm in the rabbit-placing business.

But first, I need to find where Consort hides his stash of industrial-strength allergy medication.

HE'S A REBEL 'CAUSE HE NEVER EVER DOES WHAT HE SHOULD

So yeah, the rabbit. He's been here a week now. Until two days ago, I began all conversations with "You want a rabbit?" To absolutely no one's surprise, not one single person has responded with "*DO* I!"

During the day, he runs around our yard. At night, I put him in the dog-crate and place him in the garage so he won't be bothered (which it to say, eaten) by nighttime yard critters. He has fresh hay, fresh water, more-or-less fresh vegetables. I wear gardening gloves when handling the hay. It's not been the ideal, but were I a rabbit, I'd call it a reasonable Plan B. Rupert barked at him and chased him exactly once, after which I spoke to him sharply. He wilted and has let the rabbit alone ever since. When looking for your next dog, make sure to inquire if the dog shames easily; I tell you, it's a Godsend. The cats aren't allowed out, but they have taken to sitting in the kitchen window, watching the bunny hop around outside. This provides hours of entertainment. The windows are their television and, apparently, I just ordered premium cable.

What's he like, this bunny? Depends. If he's in the back yard, he's fairly indifferent to us, periodically opting to sit next to whoever is on the chaise, making a big show of eating clover and looking in the opposite direction, being a jaded little lagomorph who only *appears* to want some petting. Then he gets petted for a few minutes and appears to like it. Then he lunges off. If the petter happens to be me, I go inside and scrub my hands up to my armpits like a surgeon.

But once he goes to the dog run behind the garage, he's a very, very, VERY different little man. The dog run BELONGS TO THE RABBIT. All who enter MUST ANSWER FOR THEIR BEHAVIOR!

The dog run attaches to the yard by way of a path behind the garage and any surveyor would tell you it's all of a single parcel.

THE SURVEYOR WOULD BE WRONG FOR THE BACK YARD BELONGS TO THE RABBIT AND OTHERS, BUT THE DOG RUN BELONGS SOLELY TO THE RABBIT. IF YOU COME TO THE DOG RUN, THE RABBIT WILL RUN IN CIRCLES AROUND YOU UNTIL YOU LEAVE.

You're thinking *Awwww* right now. *How cute.* That's okay. I thought that, too, until yesterday.

It was midafternoon. I saw no rabbit in the back yard. I went to the dog run and called "Rabbit?" A small face peeked out from behind the gate. Having established he wasn't missing, I turned to leave the back yard when I heard a crashing. Turning, I saw the rabbit streaking through the grass towards me. Expecting the usual circling-until-I-left, I took a step backward. He lunged for my ankle. Stupidly, I put my hands down to shoo him away.

He bit my hand. Hard.

I pried his jaw off my hand. He took this opportunity to bite the other hand. I held up my hand; the rabbit hung from it for a few seconds like an ornament, then dropped off and lunged for me again. I sprinted for the back door, losing a sandal in the process. I stood inside the screen door and panted, eyeing my abuser. The rabbit sniffed the abandoned flip-flop disinterestedly and found a grass-blade worthy of him. The scene was pastoral. Were it not for the rabbit-tooth divots in my hand, I'd have thought I'd hallucinated the whole episode.

Don't worry, Mom. He didn't break the skin. Two Benadryl later, the swelling came down. A little online research and a quick call to the woman who handles the bunnies at our rescue told me what I had suspected: testosterone is a very powerful drug. Once he's neutered, he'll probably become less territorial.

Probably.

Or he's just a bit of a jerk.

So next week, this bunny gets snipped. It'll come out of my pocket, because there is no municipal program to underwrite rabbit-neutering. Maddeningly, neutering a rabbit costs more than neutering a dog or a cat. This has something to do with the size of the parts and added complexity of working in confined spaces. Anyway, after that I'll try to place him again, but I'm starting to think he's going to live in our dog run for a while. I'm not happy about this, but as of this morning I've decided what he is in my life. He's my Bengali tea-boy.

Of course, I'll explain.

A friend who is a long-practicing Buddhist told me the following story: There was a highly respected Lama who was travelling the world, giving dharma lectures. This revered Master had a small entourage of assistants and apostles, including a tea-boy from Bengal who went everywhere with him. This tea-boy was incompetent, rude to the Lama and his students, and a general chore to have around. Many people, assuming the Lama was too kind, or too evolved, to fire the dreadful tea-boy, offered to do this job instead. The Lama refused. He kept the boy because he operated in a world where everyone wanted to make things easy on him, but the Lama understood that the boy provided a constant incentive to practice patience and non-judgment. Every religion on earth stresses the importance of treating others with patience, kindness and mercy. The followers of these religions also know how difficult the practice of patience, kindness, and mercy can be on a daily basis.

It's easy to love a dog that worships us and corrects his behavior after a single sharp tone. It's easy to love the cats that make doe-eyes at us, and make us laugh and snuggle us to sleep. I took on the responsibility of seeing to the welfare of an animal that didn't ask to be small and helpless, and can't help having the personality of a *Jersey Shore* cast member after a bad night. I didn't want this rabbit, and I can't say I exactly like this rabbit, but I will care for him and love him as best as I can. His water will be clean, his hay plentiful. He will have vegetables and all the dog-run privileges he wants.

But make no mistake, those nuggets are coming off.

IF HE HEARS, HE'LL KNOCK ALL DAY

In the event I am ever unable to locate my cats — even after shaking the dry food bag and *even* after opening a can of tuna — I will not worry, because I will always have one failsafe method to find them:

I will go into my bathroom. Once inside, I will shut the door behind me, open one or more of the faucets and remove one or more elements of my clothing. Within ninety seconds, there will be ten or twenty pounds of cat slamming (SLAM) against (SLAM) the (SLAM) door (SLAM-SLAM-SLAM-SLAM).

This will also be followed by peals of agonized wailing, not all of which will originate from me. Eventually, the door will burst open and the forbidden felines will barrel in, looking at me reproachfully for having invaded their tiled sanctum without approval. If history is any indication, they will look at my undressed parts in a vaguely nauseated way and start speed-bagging the toilet paper.

If I ever go to the bathroom and find myself left alone for more than six minutes, I will have them declared legally dead.

MAD AS RABBITS

To the surprise of absolutely no one: the rabbit is still here. It is a fact of life that nearly everyone who wants a rabbit already has a rabbit. One person kindly wrote in after the first rabbit post and put me in touch with a person who actually *wanted* a rabbit. We spoke. She seemed lovely on the phone. She wanted a rabbit. Unfortunately, she lives two hours away and I felt morally obligated to do a home-check without feeling the motivation to travel two hours each way to actually conduct it. The rabbit remains here and will do so until the right home comes up — the right home within a sixty-mile radius, that is.

After the first month, I had his testicles removed. Overnight, he became a much more sociable yard-mate. I've had dogs and cats neutered before but I've never seen such a complete about-face in personality. Where there was jerkiness, there is now charm. Where he used to bite the hands that feed him, he now sidles up to say hello. And there's also his endless fascination with joyous, if pointless, hopping around. I'm so pleased with the outcome of this particular operation that it keeps coming up in conversation. I've told several people that the world would be a better place if we were allowed to cram nearly all domesticated males in a cage and take them to the vet. On what I'm sure is a completely unrelated matter, Consort no longer allows me near his friends.

But this guy was still a temporary guest (the rabbit, not Consort) and you could tell that because he still had no name. Experience has shown that when you name an animal you're one step away from the monogrammed Christmas stocking. So, for the first two months he was Rabbit or Bunny. Sometimes, if I felt like referencing *Calvin & Hobbes*, he'd be Mr. Bun. Then, just this week, as I was putting his newly equable self into his crate for the evening, I looked at his face and thought: *you look like a dentist.* I don't know exactly why, but something about his face made me want to lean into a bowl and spit. Trust me, he looks like a dentist. In that instant, Mr. Bun became Dr. Bun.

Then, Dr. Bunnerman.

Then, Dr. Bunstein.

Eventually, we settled on Dr. Marvin K. Bunstein, DDS.

The K is for Kenneth, should anyone ask. And they do.

But he's not very formal so he usually answers to "Dr. B". Unless, of course, he's feigning death.

One afternoon, Consort went out to the garage for something and left the side door ajar. Since Dr. B has always shown an unwholesome fascination with the garage and its enticing inner regions, Consort needed to make sure the rabbit hadn't snuck inside. He scanned under the workbench and behind the shelves but Dr. B was nowhere to be seen. Still, he needed to be sure, lest the bunny become a means to measure tire tread-wear.

He called for the rabbit in all of his favorite places out in the yard, then the obscure places, finally searching the far dusty corner behind the utility shed and the compost barrels. There was Dr. B, lying on his back, quite inert, a fly buzzing over one slightly opened eye. He touched the rabbit gently with his foot. Nothing. Consort winced. Something had killed the rabbit and it was best taken care of before his girls came home. He grabbed a shovel from the shed and gently scooped under the rabbit; at which point Dr. Bunstein leapt three feet in the air, dashed the length of the yard, panting in terror and glaring at Consort over his offended but very much alive shoulder. As Consort told the story later: "Even that *fly* thought he was dead."

It seems Dr. Bunstein is just an incredibly sound midday sleeper. La siesta de la muerte. Since that day, we've all seen the death-nap. I've rolled trashcans past him without waking him up. This makes no sense considering how, in the wild, he's nothing but white meat and four potential key rings. What Darwinian force evolves defenseless prey so unaware of its surroundings? Platypuses and Komodo Dragons are one thing, but I'm guessing Darwin never met a real bunny.

So we now know he's attractive, amiable and a sound sleeper. What else can I tell you? Oh, right...He's an idiot. Someone had to graduate at the bottom of bunny class and it might have been my furry dentist. Of course, we need to consider the job specs of a rabbit:

1. Eat vegetables.

2. Poop.

3. Make more rabbits.

I'll never know how he fared with numbers two and three, but man is he feeble at number one. I'll walk out to the backyard carrying a clump of broccoli, a vegetable we've determined delights him to no end. Dr. B hears my footsteps and dashes out from some shady spot. We rendezvous at his food corner, where he always gets his food. He circles my feet three or four times in delight because this is where food is served. I put the broccoli down at my feet, right next to him. Dr. B stares at me blankly.

DR. B: Food?

QUINN: Right there. Next to you.

Dr. B daintily steps over the broccoli and inspects my foot.

DR. B: We're in the food corner! Food?

Quinn picks up Dr. B and turns him so his head is directly facing the broccoli. Dr. B steps on the broccoli, turns around and looks up hopefully.

DR. B: Give me a hint.

Sure, he may be a dim bulb but he did have the cunning to find the one house in a twelve-block radius with a human who would take him in. And he's very sweet. And utterly harmless. And it's nice to have a dentist in the family.

FIGHT THE POWER

Consort has opinions about my cat-blogs. More accurately, he has *one* opinion: I write too many cat blogs. When he comes into the office and finds me writing, he'll sneak a glance over my shoulder and sigh "Oh. CAT-blog." Having the seasoned ear of someone who has spent a decade parsing Consort-speak, I can tell you what this means:

"...Quinn, my presence in this house prevents you from being the genial-yet-obsessive pet-hoarder you long to be. But people who write about their cats all the time are only two steps above cat-ladies whose floors eventually collapse from soaked-in urine. The next step down that path includes women who possess an all-cat wardrobe. Please don't make me the guy who shows up at a dinner party with a woman wearing a sequined-kitten sweater..."

I answer this unspoken condemnation with a dismissive wipe of my tape-roller over my hoodie [this being the *office* tape-roller, as opposed to the several *closet* tape-rollers and the under-lauded *car* tape-roller]. "We're not overrun by pets," I explain to no one in particular as I massage the roller over an especially stubborn shag-rug of pet fur on my forearms; everyone knows we're the bosses around here.

I'd de-fur my lap while sitting here at the computer but, of course, Squeakers is perched there. Because I sit at the computer on one of those inflated rubber exercise balls in a futile attempt to strengthen my abs—and avoid what a friend calls "blogger-butt"—you'd think I wouldn't have a lap. Squeakers would beg to differ. There's one thigh here and another thigh there. Legally, somewhere in-between is a lap, even if the knees happen to be a foot apart. If the gently shifting ball makes me constantly readjust my center of gravity well, that's what claws are for. It's as if we've domesticated a box of syringes.

I cut her nails. I swear I do. It's just that during those vast stretches of time when I'm guilty of selfish behaviors such as not opening cans of wet food, Squeakers runs off and gets a mani-pedi at some undisclosed government instillation where the top-secret honing methods include lasers and industrial-strength diamonds. She cuts through my corduroy legs like room-temperature cheese.

It's not mean, though. Oh, howdy, it's not mean. Diana likes me well enough, but Squeakers wants us to move to a more tolerant country where we can finally make it legal. For the first year—in recognition of Consort's allergy to cats and his incredible patience when it comes to my irrational devotion for pets—the rule was NO CATS IN THE BEDROOM EVER. We all understand that meant every time the bedroom door was opened even a crack, a feline would fly into the room as if launched from a giant slingshot, run for the bed, and jettison a cubic yard of fur. Within months Consort, who knows a lost cause when he sees one, amended the rule: They can visit during the day, but the air-purifier runs at all times. And no sleeping there at night.

Truly, that would have been the end of it, were it not for the fact that when I wake up in the night—either because nature or Daughter calls—I am never awake enough to remember "Say, between me and the place I want to go is a closed door." The first, full face-plow into an oak door at 3:30 a.m. had a certain graceless charm if you like hurling obscenities into the darkness. And bruising. By the eighth midnight demonstration of moving-human-force meets opposable-building-object, things needed to change. The air-purifier was ratcheted up to turbo and the cats slept where they liked. No more zombie-walk nose jobs occurred and peace reigned.

Well, sort of. The air-purifier now runs at a volume slightly above a jet engine revving for takeoff. This must have bothered Squeakers delicate feline ears, because she established a new policy: *I sleep under the covers, next to my beloved, the one with the perforated lap.* Consort came in one night to the sight of my sitting up in bed reading. Sprawled next to me was Squeakers, spooning me from the middle of the mattress, one leg stretched protectively across my abdomen. She was snoring softly.

"They've won, you know," he said conversationally.

"Of course they haven't won," I whispered. "They're pets. We still have the final vote around here. Now get into bed quickly, because she doesn't like when the quilt moves and the cold air gets in."

I think he mumbled something about a sequined sweatshirt but it was hard to hear over the air-purifier.

And the purring.

* * *   * * *   * * *

ACKNOWLEDGEMENTS

Heartfelt thanks to Bobby Owsinski for putting this idea in my head to begin with and then helping us build the infrastructure. "I couldn't have done it without you" is such a cliché but this time, it happens to be true.

Thanks to my mother for, among things too numerous to mention here, teaching me that pets were always worth the mess, (and also having kept our family pictures carefully labeled so I could locate the snapshot on the cover).

Thanks to Daughter, the sharpest copy editor ever to have borrowed my shoes.

Mostly, thanks to Consort for doing every single non-writing task related to this book and for always saying "Sure" whenever I show up with another pet. He is the best of all good eggs and every time I find him trying to sleep while a cat inserts her tail up his nostril, I love him that much more.

Finally, thanks to *Swiffer*, *Furminator* and any company that makes adhesive lint-rollers.

ABOUT THE AUTHOR

Quinn Cummings is an Oscar-nominated actor (*The Goodbye Girl, Family*), and a critically acclaimed author and humorist whose previous books, *Notes from the Underwire* and *The Year of Learning Dangerously*, have earned a new generation of fans worldwide. She writes the popular blog, *The QC Report*, where many of these essays first appeared. Her writing has appeared in The Atlantic, Time, Newsweek, The Wall Street Journal, Los Angeles Magazine, Good Housekeeping, and many other publications. She lives in Los Angeles with her partner and their daughter.

Visit on the web at **www.QuinnCummings.com**
Follow her on Twitter: **@quinncy**
On Tumblr: **quinncummings.tumblr.com**

———

Jacket design:
Mark Harvey / fluxion.net

Cover photograph © Cummings Family Archive
Photograph of the author © Clyde Smith

QUINELLA
MEDIA USA

40919309R00129

Made in the USA
Lexington, KY
03 June 2019